AMERICANA LIBRARY

ROBERT E. BURKE, EDITOR

Spending to Save

THE COMPLETE STORY OF RELIEF

By HARRY L. HOPKINS

Introduction by Roger Daniels

UNIVERSITY OF WASHINGTON PRESS
SEATTLE AND LONDON

Library of Congress Cataloging in Publication Data
Hopkins, Harry Lloyd, 1890–1946.
    Spending to save.
    (Americana library, AL–23)
    Includes bibliographical references.
    1. Unemployed—U. S.   2. U.S. Federal Civil Works
Administration.   3. U. S. Federal Emergency Relief
Administration.   4. U.S. Work Projects Administration.
    5. Public welfare—U. S.   I. Title.
HV91.H6   1972   361.6'2   79-172902
ISBN 0-295-95182-6

To

BARBARA DUNCAN HOPKINS

CONTENTS

FOREWORD

During the years from 1929 to 1932 we saw our national income fall from eighty-one billion to thirty-nine billion dollars a year. Few people are able to visualize the meaning of the words national income. If they conjure up any picture, it is of a golden cataract of dollars falling into one specific place like the United States Treasury. Its stoppage seems as abrupt and dramatic as would the diversion of the Niagara River above the Falls. This concept is far from true. When the national income recedes, it dries up like the waters of many wells. In the spring of 1933, the well had gone completely dry for one out of every six families in the land.

In the last three and a half years we have spent almost six billion dollars in helping these families to maintain themselves. What we bought with our money is told in the pages of this book. How much this six billion dollars has served to deter the further decline of the national income is a matter of opinion. Certainly it has had the widest, if by the same token the thinnest, spread of purchasing power of any other six billion dollars in the sum total of the national livelihood. That it has been spent honestly and with constant remembrance of its purpose, that it has bought more of courage than it ever bought of goods, is due to the un-

1

tiring energies of devoted men and women who, in every city and county in the United States, have helped to administer relief. To them I should like to express my gratitude.

INTRODUCTION

Harry Lloyd Hopkins was born, the fourth of five children in a middle-class family, in Sioux City, Iowa, on 17 August 1890; he died, fifty-six years later, a world figure, in New York City. During his childhood the family lived in several midwestern states, following the elder Hopkins' changing and not too successful business pursuits; eventually the family settled in Grinnell, Iowa, a college town of five thousand. He, like all his brothers and his sister, attended Grinnell College and was graduated in 1912. In that year fewer than forty thousand Americans were graduated from college, although the nation's population was over ninety-five million. Hopkins was a "big man" on the Grinnell campus and lettered in basketball; he was a political science major but did not excel academically. It is interesting to note that, in addition to Hopkins, four others who became significant New Dealers were graduated from Grinnell between 1910 and 1913: Chester C. Davis, head of the Agricultural Adjustment Administration; Paul H. Appleby, long-time assistant to Henry A. Wallace, who became undersecretary of agriculture; and two women who worked for Hopkins, Florence S. Kerr, assistant commissioner of both the Works Progress Administration and the Federal Works

Agency, and Hallie Flanagan, director of the Federal Theater Project of the WPA.[1]

After graduation Hopkins found his way, rather by accident, into social work. It is usually noted that Edward A. Steiner, a professor of sociology at Grinnell, arranged a summer job for him with Christodora House, a well-known New York settlement; but perhaps an even more important influence was his older sister Adah (Mrs. Frank Aime), who had been converted from library science to social work by Jane Addams, and was, at that time, registrar of the School for Philanthropy in New York.[2] Whatever the reason for his career choice, Hopkins quickly rose to the top. He soon found a regular job with the Association for Improving the Condition of the Poor, and in 1915 he became executive secretary of New York City's Board of Child Welfare. He served the American Red Cross as director of regional offices in New Orleans and Atlanta from 1917 to 1922, and then became director of the New York Tuberculosis and Health Association. Rather than the "obscure social worker"— a description in which he reveled—Hopkins was, in 1931, a well-known social-work executive earning in excess of ten thousand dollars a year, a larger salary than he would command during his New Deal heyday.

His government career began in 1931, when he was "loaned" by the Tuberculosis and Health Association to the New York State Temporary Emergency Relief Administration (TERA) to be executive director under

1. "Grinnellians in the New Deal," *The Grinnell Magazine*, Vol. 1, No. 1 (Winter 1967-68), pp. 3-10. I am indebted to my colleague, Bruce Pauley, for bringing this article to my attention.
2. Interview with Mrs. Frank Aime, August 1967.

Jesse Isidor Straus (of the Macy Department Store Strauses), who served as figurehead chairman until 1932, when Hopkins took over the top spot. The TERA job lasted until he went to Washington in May 1933, but it produced no close association with New York's governor, Franklin D. Roosevelt. TERA headquarters were in New York City rather than Albany, and the governor and his emergency relief director saw each other little. By the end of April 1933, after eighteen months of operation, the TERA had, under Hopkins' supervision, spent $136,954,952 of state funds, largely in home and work relief. In his last full month on the job, there were 412,882 relief cases in the TERA's books.[3]

Hopkins' appointment, in May 1933, as federal relief administrator, was a logical one. In his New York State job he had dispensed more relief money than anyone in American history, although, of course, the federal spending he was to supervise would soon dwarf that. In the five years that he was in charge of federal relief, Hopkins was responsible for spending some nine billion dollars. The true magnitude of that figure may not readily be apparent in the light of massive contemporary federal spending; but total federal expenditure for essentially the same period—fiscal years 1934 through 1939—was "only" about forty-five billion dollars, so that federal relief accounted for about twenty cents in every dollar. In the process of spending, Hopkins, of course, established himself as perhaps *the* pre-eminent New Dealer. As Raymond

3. Temporary Emergency Relief Administration, *Five Million People One Billion Dollars: Final Report of the Temporary Emergency Relief Administration*, Albany, N.Y., 1937.

Clapper put it toward the end of 1937:

Most of those young, daring, and active New Dealers who mobilized in Washington in the spring of 1933 have succumbed to weary, disillusioned middle age. Some of them have left. . . . Others . . . have just grown tired. They have discovered that making America over is a discouragingly slow and tedious task. . . . But none of this is true of Harry Hopkins. He is going to see it through. . . . In four and a half years of federal relief, Hopkins has been the object of more criticism and controversy than all other New Dealers combined. You might think that by now his sharp-jutting chin would have been worn away by what it has had to take. Yet it is sticking out strong as ever, ready for more. He has learned that some things just can't be done. But he is convinced still that many things can be done. So he isn't quitting. On the contrary, he has his second wind.[4]

Hopkins left his relief job in 1938 to become secretary of commerce for a little over a year. For a time, he was believed to be Roosevelt's designated successor, and he probably at least half believed it himself. After 1940, when he helped engineer Roosevelt's unprecedented third-term nomination, Hopkins, like his chief, converted to war. For the rest of Roosevelt's administration, though he held few official posts and none of high rank, he was the president's trouble-shooter and right hand, going on arduous missions to England and the Soviet Union and living much of the time in the White House. Robert Sherwood has chronicled those years well in *Roosevelt and Hopkins*. From 1938 on, Hopkins was often seriously ill with stomach and intestinal problems, exacerbated by a man-killing

4. Raymond Clapper, "Who Is Hopkins?" *Forum*, December 1937.

schedule, and his last years were punctuated by periods spent in the Mayo Clinic. He died, exhausted, on 29 January 1946, just nine months after his beloved chief.

Although he made countless speeches and published a number of articles, *Spending to Save* is the only book to bear Hopkins' name. It is obviously a staff production, for it contains none of the personal trademarks— such as a wise-cracking introduction—that mark almost all of his speeches, as delivered. It can be taken, however, as an accurate representation, as of 1936, of Hopkins' views on what we now call the welfare state. The chief significance of the book is that it presents the mature views of one of the major architects of American social policy.

Most social workers, in the years before the great depression, were dedicated to case work. Their basic assumption was that poverty, or failure to function adequately within the system, was essentially the fault of the individual rather than the system. In part, at least, Hopkins understood, long before most of his contemporaries, that national problems required national solutions. As early as 1914, in the depression that preceded World War I, he called for the establishment of a national employment bureau.[5] As TERA director he constantly urged the state and local governments to combat the depression by spending more for relief rather than applying the traditional wisdom of curtailing expenditures.[6] Although his views were quite advanced, Hopkins, even in mid-1933, had no clear idea of the magnitude or the duration of the depression. In a memorandum that he

5. *New York Times*, 3 February 1914.
6. Ibid., 8 June 1932.

prepared for the French writer André Maurois, after a little more than a month in his federal job, Hopkins wrote:

The question is, how long is this thing going to last? What are these recovery measures doing for [the unemployed]? I don't think anybody can go on year after year, month after month accepting relief without affecting his character in some way unfavorably. It is probably going to undermine the independence of hundred[s] of thousands of families, and it is going to cost this enormous sum of money for years to come.

I believe that this public works thing, which is one feature of this plan, will put one million men to work before fall. The Federation of Labor figures twelve million unemployed to go to work. It is all merely a guess, nobody knows. One million men for public works,—Johnson figures one and one-half million—I think we may put four or five million to work by next Fall. Many people think that does the trick, but it does not. It will still leave seven million, a perfectly staggering figure to think of. I really haven't any idea what's going to happen to this relief picture. My friends say it will take five years. Senator LaFollette thinks this is good for five years. I hate to think so. One reason I am not going to build it up is for fear that it might last. I look upon this as a great disaster and wish to handle it as such. I like to think that we were through this and I have got these people into the conviction that we can do this trick. The President is realistic and is not afraid to look facts in the face. His whole future depends on putting people back to work. His immediate success depends upon it. Putting people back on real jobs is a lot bigger matter since the depression started . . . certainly in the steel business they are never going to employ as many men as before, and this may be true of many industries.[7]

7. "Résumé of Discussion on Relief," memorandum from Hopkins to André Maurois, 27 June 1933, Harry L. Hopkins Papers, Franklin D. Roosevelt Library, Hyde Park, N.Y. He refers to Senator Robert M. La Follette, Jr., of Wisconsin, and to Hugh S. Johnson, then head of the National Recovery Administration.

As this excerpt should make clear, Hopkins, despite his innovative approach to many problems, held certain assumptions about federal relief that were quite similar to those held by Herbert Hoover and other Social Darwinists. It is also interesting to note his early advocacy of the "stagnationist" philosophy that was to loom so large in the approach of most New Dealers. By 1936 his views had evolved; instead of hoping that the depression and chronic unemployment could be coped with quickly, he was beginning to envision a kind of permanent WPA to take up the slack between those whom private industry could employ and the total labor force, a system in which the federal government would become a kind of employer of last resort.

Thirty-five years have passed since Hopkins wrote *Spending to Save*, and some of its lessons, at least, have not yet been absorbed into the American consensus. Despite all the built-in stabilizers of the welfare state, unemployment hovers at about 6 percent of the labor force, a lower figure than in any New Deal year but far too high for an affluent society. Under the slogan of a "new federalism," the national administration is proposing to turn back to the states the primary responsibility for unemployment and poverty. Hopkins' book, then, is more than a vital document of a bygone crisis; it has at least something to contribute toward the solution of contemporary problems.

ROGER DANIELS

Fredonia, New York
August 1971

SPENDING TO SAVE

CHAPTER I

THE RISE OF UNEMPLOYMENT *

FOR SOME months before the dramatic crash of speculative values on the New York Stock Market there had
been signs of increasing distress in the United States.
In the spring of 1929, in many places and in many
industries, men and women who depended for their
living upon their jobs were finding it harder to retain
those jobs and much harder to find new ones. By March,
1929, there were 2,860,000 unemployed men and women
in the United States, according to the estimates of Robert R. Nathan of the President's Committee on Economic Security. Underneath the surface, a prosperity
built on illusory values and incomplete distribution of
its benefits had begun to decline. The majority of the
population had but limited means of obtaining accurate
information concerning the true status of their security.
The leaders of industry and government had become
accustomed to the inevitable beneficence of good times,

* All figures are from *Estimates of Unemployment in the
United States, 1929-1935* by Robert R. Nathan. International
Labour Office. Geneva. 1936.
The estimates of unemployment used in this book were prepared by Robert R. Nathan for the President's Committee on
Economic Security. There are no official government estimates
of unemployment but several organizations have prepared estimates. In addition to the Nathan estimates, the National Research League, the Alexander Hamilton Institute, the Cleveland Trust Company, the American Federation of Labor and
the National Industrial Conference Board have prepared unemployment estimates. The estimates show the peak of unemployment to have been reached in March, 1933, ranging from the

13

and it was distinctly unpleasant for them even to contemplate the possible end of a perfect day.

Then, like a destructive cloudburst, the fierce liquidation of October and November, 1929, occurred on the New York Stock Exchange. The mad scramble to sell securities, which only a few days before had been regarded as priceless, affected the lives and happiness of millions of people who had thought they had no direct connection with such things. Unemployment increased to nearly 3,000,000 in December of that year. Still the people and their leaders could not grasp the full significance of what had happened to them. They were too close to the picture to be able to see it in proper focus.

On November 21, 1929, President Hoover met with some of the leaders of business and industry, and after this meeting he asked Julius H. Barnes, president of the Chamber of Commerce of the United States, "to create an Executive Committee from members of this group and the various trade organizations who could assist in expansion of construction and maintenance of employment." Representatives of trade associations and business leaders held a large conference on December 5, 1929, strongly endorsed the movement and pledged their cooperation. The following objectives were developed at this conference:

National Research League estimate of 17,920,000 to the National Industrial Conference Board estimate of 13,300,000.

These various estimates of unemployment follow similar general methods of computation. They are all derived from employment data. The total number of gainful workers is computed from 1930 Census data kept up-to-date by adjustment for the estimated increase in the working population. Then the total number of persons estimated from current employment series to be actually working is deducted from the estimated number of gainful workers. The remainder is the number of workers estimated to be unemployed.

"(1) Promotion of prudent public and private construction through trade associations and chambers of commerce, in cooperation with the Department of Commerce.

"(2) Stimulation of repairs, replacements and betterments in industrial and business plants and in the home.

"(3) Development of normal prudent purchasing and placing of advance orders through cooperation of retail and wholesale trade associations and sales forces.

"(4) The setting-up of an information service to aid in the above and any other measures that might be found desirable and to disseminate accurate facts regarding the business situation and off-set unfounded rumors."

Meanwhile, government officials and the executives of industry attempted to reassure a bewildered people. "Prosperity," they told the press and the public, "is just around the corner." If only the people would not worry too much, if only employers would keep their employees on payrolls, this temporary storm would pass, and all would be well. But employers themselves were worried and finding it difficult to meet their payrolls without digging into past profits. Gradually salaries and wages were reduced, and men and women were silently disappearing from payrolls and calculating with increasing alarm the remaining balances in their savings accounts.

The National Business Survey Conference, operating through the Chamber of Commerce of the United States, continued during the first months of 1930 to distribute information to local chambers of commerce concerning the plans for employment stabilization in various communities throughout the country. More and more men and women were losing their jobs and consuming their savings. By January, 1930, it was estimated that there were 4,065,000 unemployed in the United States. In February there were 4,424,000; in March 4,644,000; in April 4,386,000; in May 4,299,000; in June 4,161,000; in July 4,196,000; in August 4,782,000; in September 5,040,000; in October 5,481,000.

Government leaders and some industrial leaders were urging employers not to cut payrolls or discharge workers. But this request was equivalent to asking them to change the entire business structure of the United States into a philanthropic machine, to assume the responsibility for their workers, and to pay wages out of diminishing profits. As the payrolls decreased, the sales of both luxuries and necessities went down, while construction of new factory buildings, railroad improvements, apartment houses and farm developments was curtailed.

Finally, on October 17, 1930, President Hoover issued a statement revealing that he had that day requested Secretary of Commerce Lamont, Secretary of Labor Davis, Secretary of the Interior Wilbur, Secretary of the Treasury Mellon, and Governor Eugene Meyer of the Federal Reserve Board, "to formulate and submit to me plans continuing and strengthening the organization of Federal activities for employment during the winter."

In his statement President Hoover said: "There are three directions of organization in which the Federal government activities can cooperate. First, Cooperation with the governors and employment organizations of the states and local communities; second, development of methods with the national industries; and third, in direct Federal employment in public works, etc." The President then recalled that he had set up ten months previously "arrangements which have continued since that time, and which have contributed greatly to reduce unemployment." He was referring to the National Business Survey Conference, which did nothing but send information to chambers of commerce in various states. President Hoover then went on to praise the committees for unemployment relief which had been set up in some states. He said that he had been in communication with some of the governors in order to get their views of methods by which the Federal government might supplement "assistance to their organizations." His new Cabinet Committee, he said, would "again seek the cooperation of our business leaders and our national industries which we have had on so generous a scale during the past year." President Hoover ended his statement with these words: "As a nation we must prevent hunger and cold to those of our people who are in honest difficulties."

But it was discovered that cooperation with industrial leaders and the pious wish to prevent hunger and cold to those of the people who were in honest difficulties were not enough. Previously President Hoover, according to the statement of E. P. Hayes, one of his subsequent unemployment advisers, had been reluctant to form even a committee for unemployment relief, "being fearful that such action would tend to magnify the emergency in the mind of the public." Finally, however, on October 21, 1930, a statement was issued from Washington that Colonel Arthur Woods of New York had been appointed to deal with the unemployment situation. No program was laid down for Colonel

Woods, and the status of his committee was doubtful. During the first days of his work he was known
as "Director General of Unemployment." One of his
advisers was Edward L. Bernays, public relations counsel. When it came time to choose a name for Colonel
Woods' organization, Mr. Bernays suggested that "Employment" rather than "Unemployment" should be
stressed. The name finally chosen was "President's
Emergency Committee for Employment." The Committee held its first meeting on October 21st, and after-
wards the press was informed that Colonel Woods had
been chosen to establish a nation-wide organization "to
help place 2,500,000 persons back to work this winter."

On November 6, 1930, Colonel Woods telephoned
to the governors of all the states in the United States
to inquire into the unemployment situation in each
state. The stenographic record of these conversations,
which reposes in the files of the Woods Committee,
indicates clearly the attitude of mind then prevalent.

The Woods Committee was not organized in order
to render Federal financial aid to the states and their local communities, but to furnish each state with the benefit of the experience of other states in coping with the
serious unemployment problem. Some of the states,
Arizona and California, for example, had a serious problem in November, 1930, because of the number of transients pouring across their borders without means for
providing for themselves, and seeking jobs which were
non-existent. Governor Phillips, of Arizona, told Colonel Woods of the serious condition among the cotton
pickers of his state. "We had one man here," Governor
Phillips said to Colonel Woods, "who picked six days,
and when he got through—they had fed him and housed

him and charged him that expense—and when he got through he only drew thirty cents."

Governor Bibb Graves, of Alabama, told Colonel Woods that the large steel plants of Birmingham were cutting down their employment rolls. In addition there had been drought in Alabama, and the agricultural counties were in serious condition. "I want, not only suggestions," Governor Graves said, "but help before these people get to suffering. I want to do something to add to their buying power and that will stimulate the whole thing."

Arkansas, too, had drought and industrial unemployment, and Governor Harvey Parnell told Colonel Woods that he did not know what would become of the agricultural population and the industrial unemployed during the coming winter. Governor C. C. Young, of California, stressed the fact that between August, 1929, and November, 1930, employment in 750 industrial establishments of California had dropped by 12.2 per cent and that wages of those still employed had decreased by 15.2 per cent. He added that the number of destitute transients flocking to California for the winter was creating a serious problem.

Governor John H. Trumbull anticipated a hard winter for Connecticut, and stated that there was "a very substantial amount of unemployment in the State." It had been estimated at from 45,000 up, he added. "I should say we are probably that and probably more." Governor William H. Adams, of Colorado, saw no signs of improvement. In Florida, Governor Doyle E. Carlton said that the state was overrun with people coming there to seek employment. The Governor of Illinois, Louis L. Emmerson, said the situation in that large industrial state was not improving, and that he had telegraphed to Secretary of War Hurley "to see if they would release some of the cots and blankets for use in the armories of Chicago." The Governors of Idaho, Indiana, Iowa, Kansas, Kentucky, Maine and Maryland reported to Colonel Woods that conditions were not very serious. The reports varied and were confused. In some states grave situations were reported, and in others there was little or no information or organization to deal with the problem. In some of the southern states drought was causing wide distress, and in some of the industrial centers there was grave difficulty. No one knew the extent of unemployment even approximately and there was no attempt made to gauge the character of the unemployed or their requirements. The national administration felt that voluntary contributions to community chests could take care of the situation. In the rural areas it was believed that the Red Cross could care for drought sufferers. Neither of these organizations, however, was able to raise sufficient funds to take care of the growing need and, in fact, in their efforts to raise money they competed with each other. Meanwhile, citizens in some parts of the country and a number of congressmen in Washington were beginning to urge a large Federal appropriation for a public works program, but the administration, and some of the state officials, frowned on Federal aid.

The Woods Committee, in an effort to get an approximation of the unemployment problem, asked the Metropolitan Life Insurance Company on November 13, 1930, to take a sample census of unemployment, as it had done in previous depressions. On December 8, 1930, the Metropolitan took a census among its policy holders, and the information, as it was finally presented to Congress on January 24, 1931, indicated that "it seems probable that the total number of wholly unemployed persons in the United States in the first week of December, 1930, was between 4,500,000 and 5,000,-000, or about 10 per cent of the total number of persons with gainful occupations." The figures of the International Labour Office report by Robert R. Nathan for December, 1930, are 6,956,000.

President Hoover was to address Congress on the State of the Union on December 2, 1930. The Woods Committee offered detailed suggestions for the President's message, in so far as it treated the unemployment problem. The suggestions began with this statement:

"You are assembled here at a time when great numbers of our fellow citizens are facing a desperate emergency. The number of unemployed runs into the millions. Even after we have made due allowance for those unemployed who constitute no pressing social problem, it is a staggering total. Even though we know that the upturn in business activity cannot long be postponed and may already be under way, the problem of the unemployed remains. That this situation should occur in the richest country of the world challenges us all.

"I do not need to dwell upon the human meaning of such a condition although I cannot entirely pass it by. Statistics are a poor vehicle with which to tell the story. If we could forget the figures and picture one single case of extreme need resulting from unemployment,—the vain search for a job, the loss of savings, the piling up of bills, the worry over the future, the break-up of the family, the pawning of furniture, the borrowings from friends, perhaps even actual physical want and loss of health, resort to antisocial pursuits for income, and,—most significant of all, the loss of hope and ambition and of faith,—then when we have multiplied this case by the number similarly affected we can begin to realize the destruction of human values through unemployment." The suggested statement for Congress went on to point out that in the depression of 1921, following the war prosperity, more than four million men were estimated to be unemployed, and that the loss in wages, "and, therefore, in purchasing power" at that time was estimated to be over six billion dollars. The Woods Committee's suggested message for President Hoover went on to state:

"The ravages of unemployment must in our minds be compared to the ravages of war or disease. It is the great blot on our economic system today.

"In short our industrial system finds itself in a grave, tragic, stupid and anomalous situation. We have abundant—seemingly superabundant—resources of raw materials, man power, manufacturing, transportation and distribution facilities. We also have a seeming plethora of fluid capital. On the one hand we have idle workers—literally millions of them—able to work, exceedingly anxious to do so, and desperately in need of the things which they might produce if they had the opportunity. On the other hand we have idle resources and idle plants which the owners very much desire to have in operation, and in many cases desperately need to have working for financial reasons; and we do not know how to bring the two together. Nobody profits by the situation; everybody loses. It seems to be nobody's fault. It has come about as the result of uncontrolled economic forces which are not well understood. . . .

"I submit that industrialists, economists and statesmen should now address themselves wholeheartedly to the correction of this stupid situation, with a fixed determination to stay on the job until it has been mastered. We must not give up until we have approached the ideal situation, namely, that every person who is honestly seeking work should be able to find suitable work, under conditions that are reasonable; and that when he has to change from one job to another, it should be possible for him to do so without reducing himself and his family to living conditions which will deteriorate them."

The Woods Committee's proposed message went on to suggest to Congress appropriations of $830,000,000 for the cooperation of the Federal government with the states in the construction of highways, needed public improvements planned but not appropriated for, and for repair and maintenance of Federal property. The suggested message also recommended programs of slum clearance and low cost housing, and a program of rural electrification. In this section the suggested message added: "We have the resources, the materials, the labor and the skill. An effort should be made to release these forces in correcting a long recognized defect and in increasing the health, safety, and beauty of our communities." The message also suggested that a large sum be placed at the disposal of the President for use in future times of business depression for a long-range program of public works. The Woods Committee also recommended that President Hoover should suggest to Congress the passage of Senator Wagner's Bill (S. 3059) providing for advanced planning in public works, with a six-year construction program. The suggested message also stated: "The volume of employment on public construction . . . will not nearly compensate for the shrinkage of employment in private industry. The largest opportunity, therefore, to deal with unemployment rests initially with our economic organization. I hope the time may come when it will bring about some tangible financial provision for employees against the day of their necessary release either permanent or temporary."

The message which President Hoover delivered to Congress on December 2, 1930, was a very different document. On the contrary he told Congress that "the fundamental strength of the Nation's economic life is unimpaired" and attributed the depression to speculative activity within our borders and to world-wide overproduction of basic commodities. Political agitation in Asia, revolutions in South America, political unrest in some European countries, "dumping" by Russia of her agricultural products, and the American drought "have all contributed to prolong and deepen the depression," the President said. He added: "In the larger view the major forces of the depression now lie outside of the United States, and our recuperation has been retarded by the unwarranted degree of fear and apprehension created by these outside forces."

President Hoover told Congress that the total of unemployment in the United States, according to the April, 1930, Census of Unemployment, was 2,500,000, despite the fact his own Committee for Employment had received the conservative estimate of the Metropolitan Life Insurance Company's later census, indicating unemployment at that time of between 4,500,000 and 5,000,000. (This census was not presented to Congress until by special resolution of January 21, 1931, it demanded the results of the Metropolitan census.) The President stated that the actual suffering was less than the estimate of 2,500,000 might lead people to believe, because individual and community efforts to supply special employment were not reflected in the indexes of statistics. He then went on to claim that the Federal government as its contribution to the problem was then engaged in "the greatest program of waterway, harbor, flood control, public building, highway, and airway improvement in all our history." He cautioned Congress that it would have presented to it numerous projects "under the guise of, rather than the reality of, their usefulness in the increase of employment during the depression." He found the total of $520,000,000, in which he included loans to shipbuilders, was "already at the maximum limit warranted by financial prudence as a continuing policy." "To increase taxation for purposes of construction work," President Hoover said, "defeats its own purpose, as such taxes directly diminish employment in private industry." President Hoover told Congress that he had canvassed the departments to find out how much added construction they could handle, and he added, cautiously, "I feel warranted in asking the Congress for an appropriation of from $100,000,000 to $150,000,000 to provide such further employment in this emergency." President Hoover's own Committee for Employment had recommended a minimum of $830,000,000 for appropriations by the Federal government for public works. Colonel Arthur Woods, head of that committee, had recommended in a memorandum dated November 11, 1930, a two billion dollar construction program by the Federal government.

At the same time individuals of prominence and persons in obscurity were suggesting plans for coping with the ever-growing problem. On December 3, 1930, Rudolph Spreckels, of 82 Wall Street, wrote to Colonel Arthur Woods concerning "the danger of encouraging idleness through charitable relief," and warning against the evils of the dole systems of England and Germany. He suggested that the administration of relief "should be placed under the control of patriotic citizens' committees with the aid of army officers experienced in housing and feeding large numbers." He added:

"Families in need of shelter, food and clothing should be cared for in quarters provided by the municipality in which they reside, in order that a careful check may be kept in their actual requirements, until they are able to secure work and become self-supporting. Single men, unable to secure work, should be enrolled at our military posts and required to drill each day. Those who are physically unable to drill, should be required to perform camp labor suitable to their age and condition of health."

Mr. John B. Nichlos, of the Oklahoma Gas Utilities Company, of Chickasha, Oklahoma, had a scheme for unemployment relief which he outlined in a letter to his friend Patrick J. Hurley, Secretary of War, on January 9, 1931. He asked that Secretary Hurley discuss his plan with President Hoover, and stated that he was trying it out in Chickasha, Oklahoma. The plan provided:

"Sanitary containers of five (5) gallons each should be secured in a large number so that four (4) will always be left in large kitchens where the restaurants are serving a volume business. The containers should be labeled 'MEAT, BEANS, POTATOES, BREAD AND OTHER ITEMS.' Someone from the Salvation Army with a truck should pick up the loaded containers every morning and leave empty ones. The civic clubs, restaurants, the proprietors and the workers should be asked to cooperate in order to take care of all surplus food in as sanitary a way as possible. In other words, when a man finishes his meal he could not, (after lighting his cigarette or cigar), leave the ashes on the food which he was unable to consume. A card should be placed in each restaurant to read as follows, 'WE WILL UTILIZE ALL SURPLUS WHOLESOME FOOD WHICH IS NOT CONSUMED FOR THE BENEFIT OF CHARITY, (or something more brief with the same meaning').

"Baskets and sacks must be placed in each store and particularly those operating meat markets. The proprietor of each firm together with the clerks will be asked to place whatever food they can spare or cannot sell. Viz. bones, meats of any kind, potatoes, apples, vegetables that might be used for soup or any other items they see fit to place in the baskets and sacks.

"All bakeries should do likewise. They should be organized and a sack or basket left at each place to pick up all the bread that cannot be sold, and also cookies and doughnuts, etc."

Ladies of the city were to volunteer their services to pick up the scrap food at the grocery stores and bakeries. The unemployed were then to work for these scrap meals by chopping wood donated by farmers. Mr. Nichlos ended his memorandum:

"We expect a little trouble now and then from those who are not worthy of the support of the citizens but we must contend with such cases in order to take care of those who are worthy. God placed them here and it is our duty to see that they are taken care of in a Christianlike manner."

Secretary Hurley sent Mr. Nichlos' plan to Colonel Arthur Woods and also spoke to the Colonel personally about the possibility of applying the plan to local communities.

Meanwhile, efforts were being made by some congressmen and their constituents to persuade the Federal administration to release its own surplus wheat and cotton for the relief of unemployment. On November 12, 1930, William G. McAdoo sent a telegram to Senator Charles L. McNary, urging that Congress authorize for the relief of the unemployed the use of 60,000,000 bushels of wheat then in possession of the Federal Farm Board. In his telegram Mr. McAdoo stated: "Already it belongs to the people and should be devoted to the relief of those who are needy and suffering." He added that after the Armistice Congress had appropriated millions to aid suffering people in Europe. Herbert Hoover, then in charge of European relief, had appeared before Congress and urged and received appropriations by the Federal government of $100,000,000 for the relief of suffering in Europe. Writing to Senator Capper on December 8, 1930, Mr. McAdoo stated:

"If 10,000,000 of our own people had been reduced to want or suffering because of some terrible cataclysm, like the Great War, or widespread pestilence, or earthquakes, or floods, or fires, their tragic condition would stir the heart and conscience of the country to such an extent that the national and state governments and private charity would respond overwhelmingly and immediately to the situation. But because these 10,000,000 people are in sore distress from an undramatic, but equally tragic cause, in its effects, their plight is not impressed upon the human mind and heart so strikingly and vividly and, therefore, neither the dimensions nor the exigency of the problem is fully appreciated. . . . Every consideration of humanity and justice demands that what belongs to the people should not be withheld from them in their hour of extremity. I am frank to say that if the government should hoard this wheat, in the face of such a situation . . . it would be an exhibition of heartlessness and callousness that could not possibly be defended."

Two days later, on December 10, 1930, Mr. J. R. McCleskey, executive director of the Economic Conservation Committee of America, who had been leading the movement for the use of the Farm Board's surplus wheat, wrote to Colonel Woods from San Francisco. Mr. McCleskey had had correspondence with President Hoover and Colonel Woods concerning the plan for some time, but without result. Mr. McCleskey wrote:

"It seems unfortunate that the President has taken a stand entirely against any form of human relief—even as a temporary expediency to mitigate actual suffering while the basic problem of industrial readjustment is being worked out—especially in view of his splendid relief work of past years and his broad sympathetic comprehension of human problems.

"We know that you will take whatever steps you can to soften the situation and help to harmonize what we all recognize to be the fundamental need of protecting the national Treasury and the temporary, but no less vital, need of binding up the wounds of those of our people who are destitute, while employment is being developed.

"It is to be hoped that the President will make this Christmas gift to the nation—it would afford as much satisfaction to the affluent class as it would relief to the destitute."

The President, however, did not make the Christmas gift of its own wheat to the nation, nor did Congress, and definite action to make use of the surplus wheat in possession of the Farm Board was not taken until March, 1932, about one year and a half later, when the situation among the unemployed had become much more acute. President Hoover approved an act on March 7, 1932, authorizing the Federal Farm Board to allot 40,-000,000 bushels of wheat to the American Red Cross. Some of this wheat was processed and sent in the form of flour to the drought areas by the Red Cross, and the rest was distributed as flour to the unemployed. On July 5, 1932, President Hoover approved an act allotting an additional 45,000,000 bushels of Farm Board wheat to the Red Cross, and on that same day the President also approved an Act of Congress allotting 500,000 bales of cotton to the American Red Cross for use in making clothing for the unemployed. On February 8, 1933, President Hoover approved an Act of Congress giving an additional allotment, not to exceed 350,000 bales of cotton, to the Red Cross. On the day before he left the White House the President approved an Act of Congress authorizing the Red Cross to exchange some of its cotton for articles containing wool.

There were complaints that the Federal government, while urging private employers to retain men on their payrolls and while asking individuals to make more work by private construction, was itself laying off men on Federal construction work in the effort to balance the budget. Watkins Overton, Mayor of Memphis, Tennessee, complained in a letter of December 13, 1930, to Lewis Meriam, a member of the President's Emergency Committee for Employment, that the Federal government was laying off men for the winter employed on Mississippi River projects. He realized, Mayor Overton wrote, that all Federal work could not be carried on vigorously during the winter, but he added that the same was true of the street department of the City of Memphis. "Frankly," Mayor Overton wrote, "it seems to me inexcusable that the Federal Government at a time like this would lay off men with nothing to support them and leave them for this city to take care of."

The War Department had issued a general order on October 18, 1930, urging the use of enlisted men wherever possible to replace civilian labor in order to economize, because of the small authorized appropriation for maintenance of buildings on army posts. The order was suspended after Colonel Woods protested to the War Department.

While Colonel Woods' Committee was carrying on a campaign through radio and newspaper advertising and publicity urging industry not to discharge men, the Gulf Oil Company, an oil company known as a Mellon company, was discharging employees. J. F. Lucey, regional director for the Southwest for the Woods Committee, sent Colonel Woods a telegram on December 13, 1930, in which he stated: "Executives are asking why I can not obtain same cooperation from Secretary of Treasury that I am obtaining elsewhere Stop Please ask Mr. Mellon use his influence requesting Gulf officials keep men on part-time where possible." Colonel Woods took the matter up with Secretary Mellon, who discussed it with the executives of his oil company by telephone. On December 15, 1930, Colonel Woods received a letter from Mr. David E. Finley, assistant to Secretary Mellon, pointing out that under the agreement entered into with President Hoover's

Cabinet Committee, all oil companies in the country were obligated to keep production down to fixed amounts. In accordance with that agreement the Gulf Oil Company had had to reduce its drilling operations in the Southwest region. Mr. Finley pointed out that it had been the policy of the Gulf Oil Company to stagger its work and share it as much as possible among its employees. The whole episode illustrates the futility of the campaign indulged in at the time in an effort to solve the growing unemployment problem by persuading industry to employ more men and to maintain payrolls. Even the valuable companies controlled by the Secretary of the Treasury, Mr. Mellon, did not feel that they could acquiesce in the requests which were made of business men by President Hoover's employment committee.

By January, 1931, there was a definite feeling among the members of the Woods Committee that the unemployment situation was going from bad to worse. At a staff meeting of the committee held on January 15, 1931, this opinion was expressed. The Red Cross had been asked to undertake drought relief in the southern states, and it was felt by members of the committee that the Red Cross should also take over unemployment relief in the small towns and rural communities of the same area. In these drought areas typhoid and pellagra were spreading, according to a report of the Surgeon General. Secretary of Agriculture Hyde refused to interpret the drought relief bill passed by Congress in such a way as to permit loans to farmers for food. Mr. Meriam, who took up the distress among farmers with the Department of Agriculture, "reported considerable quibbling over the definition of a farmer," according to the Notes on Staff Meetings of the Woods Committee.

The Department maintained that a man was not a farmer unless he farmed at least three acres. Some of the greatest distress in the drought areas was among former miners who now had small plots of ground and were engaged in raising their own food in the bituminous coal mining areas.

Several resolutions were introduced into both houses of Congress in December, 1930, calling for appropriations to aid sufferers from the drought of that year. A joint resolution calling for an appropriation of $60,000,-000 was considered. The Secretary of Agriculture, Arthur M. Hyde, was strenuously opposed to any money being appropriated for food for farmers in the drought areas. He felt that an appropriation of $25,000,-000 for loans to farmers for fertilizer, seed, feed for livestock and fuel for tractors was sufficient. Before committees of Congress he stated that to feed the farmers in the drought area would be to establish a dangerous precedent, or, as he put it, "would constitute a dangerous step toward the dole system in this country." If we began feeding drought-stricken farmers, the next thing we knew, Secretary Hyde felt, we would be feeding the unemployed in the cities. He saw no objections to feeding their work animals, fertilizing their land and fueling their tractors, but he felt that the job of feeding people was the job of the American Red Cross, which received its money from the people by voluntary contributions and not through appropriations from Congress. Some members of Congress felt that the distress in the drought areas particularly and throughout the country generally was so great that the American Red Cross should be aided in its efforts by an appropriation of $25,000,000 from Federal funds. Judge John Barton Payne, chairman of the American Red Cross, testi-

fied before a sub-committee of the House Committee
on Appropriations on January 28, 1931. He said that at
a special meeting held the day before of the Central
Committee of the American Red Cross, a resolution was
passed unanimously that the Red Cross would refuse
to undertake general unemployment relief and that the
Red Cross would refuse to accept the $25,000,000 which
the Senate had appropriated for it, and which appropriation was then being considered by the House. Judge
Payne said that he did not believe that the Red Cross
should undertake general unemployment relief, because
it did not have the necessary organization. He also felt
that this appropriation of $25,000,000 for drought relief
would interfere with the Red Cross' own efforts to raise
$10,000,000 by voluntary contributions, and he offered
figures to prove it. He added: "Why should the Government be dealing in this sort of thing when the people
have plenty of money? I do not mean to say that they
do not think they are hard up now. Many of them do.
But when they scratch the barrel, they get something."

Representative Joseph W. Byrns, in the course of the
debate on this $25,000,000 appropriation for the Red
Cross, said on the floor of the House on January 30,
1931:

> "I cannot escape the feeling, Mr. Speaker, that if
> President Hoover, fully cognizant of the distress and
> suffering which prevails throughout the entire coun-
> try—and consistent with his former record as a great
> humanitarian—had frankly admitted to the country
> the gravity of the situation as it exists today, and
> courageously declared that the suffering women,
> children, and unemployed should be taken care of,
> regardless of what might come, he would have been
> considered one of the great men in American history.

"I believe that the American people would have applauded such a stand, and I am sure that Congress would have cooperated with him in every relief measure that he might have proposed.

"I can appreciate the feeling of pride which prompts the President's desire that under his administration Congress shall not take action such as it never has been called upon to take before in the history of this Nation, and appropriate money to feed the hungry people throughout the country. I can appreciate how the Republican leaders may wish to save the administration from making that sort of a record for the Republican party. But the question, it seems to me, of relieving suffering and starving should be paramount to any feeling of pride which anyone may have and outweigh any political considerations.

"There are children. There are hungry women. There are strong men in the cities of this country who want employment and cannot secure it—and standing today with arms outstretched to Congress, appealing for relief they are asking Congress to show them as American citizens, the same sympathy and generosity it showed to foreign citizens a few years ago. No such objections as are being made now were raised when relief was being provided for those in foreign lands . . .

"There was no voice more eloquent, no person more insistent in the case of these foreign contributions than the President of the United States himself, who was then the Secretary of Commerce. If I had the time I could read to you numerous quotations from statements he made to the committee and to the country when he was appealing for these appropriations. I call attention simply to one contained in the report of the Committee of Foreign Affairs on March 3, 1924, supporting a bill to appropriate

$10,000,000 to relieve the women and children of Germany. This bill was passed by the House but failed in the Senate. What did Mr. Hoover say in his appeal to the Foreign Affairs Committee in behalf of that $10,000,000 appropriation? I quote:

" 'Our only hope is that the next generation will be better than this one, and there is no hope if they are to be stunted and degenerate from undernourishment. I recognize the many arguments that may be brought against charitable notions either by private agencies or by our Government, but I refuse to apply these arguments to children.' "

The appropriation of $25,000,000 for the Red Cross for drought and unemployment relief was finally defeated in the House in January, 1931. In March, 1931, the states appropriated $10,000,000 for the Red Cross for such relief, and this money was obtained by the process of urging state employees to give one day's pay a month to the fund. In the course of the debate in the Senate, David I. Walsh of Massachusetts said:

"This is the record we are making here. I want the country to know it, and I am ready to go to the country on that issue. I am not being fooled and I am not being deceived. Not a single bill for adequate relief will pass this Congress, and the country might as well know it, because of the determination upon the part of the administration that those who pay large income taxes and the corporation-income taxpayers of the country must not be burdened with relief obligations.

"The States and municipalities who have already incurred great expenditures for public works, who have increased tremendously their budgets for outdoor relief to the suffering, must place the tax burdens on their own unemployed and heavily burdened landowners."

In April, 1931, President Hoover officially declared the drought to be at an end, and there is this notation in the Notes on Staff Meetings of the Woods Committee, for the meeting of April 8, 1931: "A general feeling was expressed that the White House press conference, which proclaimed the drought to be officially ended, was an unwise move. It may be that this will lead to a slackening of relief measures that are still greatly needed."

The pressure of the administration and of big business at the time was against realistic treatment of the ever-growing unemployment problem. In February, 1931, according to the estimates of Robert R. Nathan, made for the International Labour Office at Geneva, there were 8,334,000 unemployed in the United States. On February 9, 1931, Mr. Rogers of the Chamber of Commerce of the United States, called on Mr. F. T. Miller of the Woods Committee, and stated that the replies to questionnaires sent out by the Chamber to its member chambers throughout the country indicated "an upturn in business." "Forty per cent, replying to the question, 'What can be done to improve the situation?' advised letting up on propaganda on unemployment." Some chambers of commerce wrote to the national chamber that they did not favor any program that advertised to the nation that there was large unemployment in their cities.

On January 27, 1931, Myron C. Taylor, chairman of the finance committee of the United States Steel Corporation, said in a radio address under the auspices of the Woods Committee:

"While the number of unemployed is considerable, the number in real distress is relatively few, because the masses have been provident and are caring for themselves and for each other. We should not overlook the fact that there are always some unemployed in each community, and this normal number should not be taken to swell the appearance of unusual distress at this time.

"To assist those less fortunately placed, the great and generous heart of our people who have enough and to spare can be depended upon to share their loaf with such as may be found to be in real need.

"One solution, and a basic one, in the adjustment of the conditions which affect the individual, is his own attitude and conduct toward life and the sincerity with which he undertakes to work. The individual with a will to work must fit himself into the new scheme of things. The slacker must give way to the man of action. The drone must not obstruct the way, or, like his prototype the bee, he will be expelled from the hive. We had almost reached the point where the many, and not the few, had concluded that they could live without work, and by their wits alone. This cannot be done. The first step for the individual is to accept that employment which lies at hand, no matter what it may be, and by his efforts and diligence and ambition to raise himself, as has been possible for others, to a better and more remunerative position. Man's field of occupation is like an ever-flowing stream; it is always moving; it can accommodate in one way or another all who are willing to work; and like all life, it is constantly discharging its burden at the end of its course, and making way for new and younger recruits at its source. The character and quality of the journey rests largely in the hands of the voyager."

This must have afforded small comfort to the thousands of miners in the bituminous coal mining areas, the thousands of drought-stricken farmers, the thousands of former bond salesmen, the thousands of worried women, who may have tuned in their radios to hear Mr. Taylor's talk. Unfortunately, at the time when Mr. Taylor spoke the number of unemployed, according to Robert R. Nathan's conservative estimates, was 8,049,000, and the number in real distress instead of "relatively few," as Mr. Taylor said, was very great, according to the testimony of social workers. It was true that the masses had been provident and were attempting to care for themselves and for each other on a sub-subsistence basis, but providence was not enough, and neither was "the great and generous heart of our people." Whatever the virtue of Mr. Taylor's philosophy of saving and thrift, more and more unemployed were every day reaching the point where there was nothing left to save. The individual with a will to work, no matter how strong that will, was finding it impossible to "fit himself into the new scheme of things." The man of action was being forced by circumstances to be a slacker. The hive had no more honey; the sources of new supply were dried up; and the industrious and thrifty were being expelled as fast and as ruthlessly as the drones. Men's wits alone were no longer effective in the desperate struggle to find work which did not exist. The individual could not "accept that employment which lies at hand," because there was no employment lying at hand, and sufficient efforts were not being made by both government and finance to stimulate jobs for the employable population by means of credit and Federal work programs. The

ever-flowing stream of man's field of occupation, which
Mr. Taylor spoke of, was drying up, and men in the
prime of life who had no resources for survival were
finding themselves abandoned, while the new and
younger recruits were still constantly coming for suste-
nance to an arid source. The character and quality of
the journey did not rest in the hands of the voyager,
but in the hands of those in government and industry
who could control the current.

By the spring of 1931 it was obvious to many of the
members of the President's Emergency Committee for
Employment that the relief need was very great, and
that it would be likely to increase rather than diminish.

Colonel Arthur Woods left the committee in May,
1931, but its activities continued under the acting chairmanship of Fred C. Croxton until August. A "Preliminary Report of the President's Emergency Committee for Employment" in the files of the Woods Committee—no final report was ever issued—stated:

> "The function of the committee was conceived of
> as being roughly analogous to that of a 'booster en-
> gine,'—an engine which is hitched on to a train
> temporarily to supplement the regular motive power
> in getting a train up an especially stiff grade."

The report went on to discuss the efforts of the Woods
Committee to see that local communities were organized
for giving employment to the unemployed, and its
propaganda efforts to urge individuals and companies
to supply employment. The entire emphasis of the
Woods Committee was on local effort, and especially
municipal effort. The committee also considered itself
a clearing house for information for employers on what
other employers were doing to stabilize employment.

A campaign was undertaken to induce individual house-holders to "clean up and fix up their homes now, in order to provide odd jobs for thousands of men." "Spruce Up" was one of the slogans of the Woods Committee. Men and women who owned homes were urged to put new roofs on them, or to make other minor repairs at once.

During the period when the Woods Committee functioned, from October, 1930, until August, 1931, the responsibility and the burden of unemployment relief were placed almost entirely on the towns, villages, cities and counties of the United States and on individuals whose instincts were philanthropic or who could be persuaded by pressure of public opinion to share their incomes, savings or wages with the more unfortunate members of their local communities. In this stage of the evolution of unemployment relief most state governments were not enlisted actively in the campaign of relief, although some of the states were spending money for relief. All through the spring of 1931 unemployment wavered around 8,000,000, according to Robert R. Nathan's estimates, but the Federal administration and the leaders of industry still insisted that the pressing needs of these people and their dependents must be met by individual philanthropy and by local public funds. The efforts of the church, the newspaper, the radio and the moving picture were enlisted in the campaign to solve the largest unemployment problem in the history of the country by means of local charity. Many leaders of business and government at the time either did not grasp, or did not wish to grasp, the magnitude of their problem. There were, perhaps, many people in 1931 who felt that Charles M. Schwab was right when he said:

"Just grin, keep on working. Stop worrying about the future and go ahead as best we can. We always have a way of living through the hard times."

But in the local communities there were millions of people who found it hard to grin, and thousands of mayors, county commissioners and village officials who found it difficult to stop worrying. Taxes could not be collected on property which was not making profits. Employment could not be furnished in factories which had no markets. The way the unemployed were living through the hard times was by scraping in garbage pails, by borrowing from one another, by sleeping in shanties, parks and fields. Thousands of others were roaming the country on foot and in old automobiles looking for work which nobody was offering.

CHAPTER II

THE DECLINE OF THE STATES

ON AUGUST 19, 1931, President Hoover announced that he had appointed Walter S. Gifford, president of the American Telephone and Telegraph Company, president of the Charity Organization Society of New York, and war-time director of the Council of National Defense, to set up a new organization "to mobilize the national, state and local agencies of every kind which will have charge of the activities arising out of unemployment in various parts of the nation this winter." After a hard winter of unemployment distress during 1930–1931 —distress which continued into the spring and summer of 1931—the Federal administration had taken one step forward at least; it had accepted the word unemployment in its vocabulary. The Gifford committee was called "The President's Organization on Unemployment Relief," whereas the Woods Committee had been called "The President's Emergency Committee for Employment." The President and Mr. Gifford in their statements began to use the distressing word "unemployment," but their attitude that the problem, however great, was one for the municipalities, counties and states remained essentially the same, with the exception that state responsibility began to be mentioned more often than previously.

A large advisory committee was set up with prominent people to act in conjunction with Mr. Gifford and his staff in Washington, in the effort to encourage local and state action for unemployment relief without committing the Federal government to financial aid. In their statements to the public and in their correspondence, Walter S. Gifford and his associates took great pains to impress upon the people of the United States that while the organization's efforts were national, the financial responsibility still remained with the states. The situation was similar to that of a wealthy individual who assured a poor relation that he would be glad to keep in touch with him by telephone and correspondence, that he would be happy to give him the benefit of his advice, but that under no circumstances must he ask his Uncle Sam for money. The Federal government had far superior sources of taxation, and could get into its treasury some of the proceeds of absentee ownership which the states and municipalities could not reach, but the Federal government in the administration of President Hoover steadfastly refused to assist the states and municipalities which were so rapidly exhausting all of their resources in the effort to take care of their destitute population.

One of the first efforts of the Gifford organization was a national drive for local contributions during the period of October 19 to November 25, 1931. Community Chest drives and Red Cross drives were to be carried on simultaneously throughout the nation during this period. The Gifford organization was careful to point out to the press and the people, however, that while this was a nation-wide drive for funds, it was not a campaign for national funds. It was designed to gain the benefits of coordination for private philanthropy without accepting Federal responsibility for the unemployment problem. Owen D. Young, who headed the Committee on Mobilization of Relief Resources, a part of the Gifford organization, pointed out in a statement at its first meeting that the funds raised would be administered and distributed in the communities where they were raised, and that "there is to be no campaign for a national fund of any character." President Hoover and his associates feared national responsibility more than they feared national unemployment, and they persistently preferred to permit the municipalities, the rural communities and the states to fall down in their efforts to take care of their unemployed adequately rather than to admit Federal responsibility for a national problem. The leaders of the Federal administration and the leaders of business alike feared that the populace would demand Federal appropriations, which would eventually result in Federal taxation to meet those needed appropriations.

When Walter S. Gifford took the chairmanship of the President's Organization on Unemployment Relief in August, 1931, Silas H. Strawn, president of the Chamber of Commerce of the United States made strenuous efforts to get important business men to act in their own states on the advisory committee which the Gifford organization set up as an adjunct to its national organization. Mr. Strawn wrote to Mr. Gifford on August 21, 1931, two days after Mr. Gifford's appointment was announced:

> "Obedient to the suggestion of the President, I have communicated with potential men in nine states; Illinois, Indiana, Maryland, Massachusetts, Michigan, New Jersey, Ohio, Pennsylvania and West Virginia. I assume that you will take care of New York yourself.
> "The purpose of my communication was to impress upon these men the necessity of prompt action

in the organization of local relief committees in order to counteract the persistent campaign for federal aid."

Almost frantic efforts were carried on during the summer and autumn of 1931 to persuade local communities to establish relief machinery which they did not have the local resources to operate effectively, so that the national administration and the large national industrial organizations could avoid the growing demand for Federal appropriations and taxation.

Irenee Du Pont wrote to Walter S. Gifford on October 6, 1931:

"Dear Mr. Gifford:—

"I have accepted a position on the Finance Committee of the Delaware relief for unemployment, passing under the style—Delaware Employment & Relief Committee.

"It will, of course, be necessary for the wealthy people of the community to contribute a considerable portion of the funds required. One of the obstacles in obtaining good contributions is the uncertainty of the tax situation. There seems to be a prevalent feeling that Congress will raise the income tax rate and remove the provision whereby losses may be offset against other income. Fear is expressed that Congress may pass a law retroactive for the calendar year 1931. In that year many wealthy people received considerable income from dividends but have met with distressing losses by the sale of securities. They must, therefore, provide liquid funds for the coming year in case such an unjust tax should be levied against them, for next year these dividends may be meagre and if the present market continues it will be nearly impossible to sell securities to meet their taxes except at staggering losses.

"I am writing you this because I feel that Mr. Hoover is very desirous that contributions to the fund should be very ample so that no suffering will result by unemployment. I think it would be very constructive if Mr. Hoover announced that no ex post facto income tax law should be passed and that he would veto a tax law if it included such an unjust provision.

"I have a personal interest in this, for I must reduce contributions next year (not on the unemployment matter but for other desirable purposes) if a high retroactive income tax law is applied but most of those that I shall have to approach are in a more serious position than I am personally.

"I have spoken to my brother, Pierre, who is on your committee, about this and think he agrees with me, but would like to put this to you at first hand.

Sincerely yours,
Irenee Du Pont"

Mr. Gifford replied on October 7, 1931:

"Dear Mr. Du Pont,
"I have your letter of October 6.
"I had already received a letter from your brother and have taken the matter up with the Secretary of the Treasury. I hope that it will be possible for some announcement to be made along the lines you and your brother suggest.

Sincerely yours,
Walter S. Gifford"

The demands throughout the country and in Congress for direct Federal financial aid were growing more persistent during the summer of 1931. William Randolph Hearst, through his newspapers, advocated a $5,000,000,000 Prosperity Loan to provide work relief for the millions of the unemployed. This plan was endorsed in resolutions sent to President Hoover by labor unions and municipalities in various parts of the country. These resolutions urged President Hoover to call a special session of Congress for the purpose of taking action on this $5,000,000,000 Prosperity Loan. On July 29, 1931, for instance, the Mayor's Unemployment Committee of Detroit, Michigan, sent to President Hoover a petition which began:

> "The present situation of depression and unemployment has created an abnormal condition in our country, amounting in effect to a crisis and a national calamity, resulting in real want, privation and even destitution for many of our people and the inevitable destruction of the moral, mental and physical condition of those affected."

After pointing out that the City of Detroit had expended large sums of money for the relief of its unemployed, this petition added:

> "The imminence of another winter of unprecedented deprivation through unemployment finds Detroit as determined as ever that no man, woman or child shall lack the elemental needs of food, clothing and shelter, but also finds the City less able than before to provide these necessities."

The petition went on to point out "that 19 per cent of the recipients of welfare aid were last employed by firms situated outside the geographical limits of the taxing power of the City of Detroit." It added that the total budget of the Detroit Community Fund, $3,600,000, was less than the expenditures made for unemployment relief by the City of Detroit during the months of February and March, 1931, alone. The petition also stated:

"Cities are limited to the conditions imposed by law in their particular States, particularly by laws governing bonding power and taxes. It is logical and necessary that the Federal Government assume leadership and organize the whole problem in order to have it centralized."

The Central Labor Union of Minneapolis, Minnesota, the Blair County Central Labor Union of Altoona, Pennsylvania, the City Council of Seattle, Washington, the New York State Federation of Labor and the City of Columbus, Ohio, endorsed the movement for Federal aid. The resolution of the City of Columbus, Ohio, dated September 15, 1931, stated:

"WHEREAS, a depression of unprecedented severity prevails and whereas winter is near and whereas at least 8,000,000 are out of employment and without means of support and are on the verge of starvation and whereas this country is threatened with pestilence, disease, crimes, riots, and political turmoil unless the needy are cared for,"

the resolution requested that President Hoover call a special session of Congress to pass an act authorizing the issuing of $500,000,000 worth of United States bonds "to provide food, clothing, fuel and shelter for the needy." The League for Independent Political Action asked President Hoover in a letter of September 4, 1931, to call a special session of Congress and ask for an appropriation of $3,000,000,000 for work relief.

During August and September, 1931, while these demands and petitions were coming into the White House from widely separated parts of the nation, President Hoover and Walter S. Gifford continued to insist on the necessity for local relief alone for the unemployed.

To bolster up this attitude President Hoover asked for opinions from the governors of some of the states. Governor Wilber M. Brucker, of Michigan, telegraphed President Hoover on August 21, 1931, and stated in his telegram: "The people of Michigan will take care of their own problem." A month before the Mayor's Unemployment Committee of Detroit had petitioned President Hoover and had pointed out that the people of Michigan could not take care of their own problem.

Governor William G. Conley, of West Virginia, writing to President Hoover on August 21, 1931, to congratulate him on the appointment of Walter S. Gifford, stated:

> "In spite of appeals that have emanated from many quarters that you convene Congress in extraordinary session to appropriate a tremendous sum of money from the Federal Treasury for relief, I feel that public opinion supports the position you have taken in opposing any step that would bring a dole system into existence in the United States. What our people need is assurance of an opportunity to earn the money to buy what they need."

Many people in West Virginia, however, had no opportunity to earn what they needed. In December, 1931, Clarence E. Pickett, secretary of the American Friends Service Committee, testified before a sub-committee of the United States Senate,* that in the spring of 1931 Fred C. Croxton of the Woods Committee (and later the assistant director of the Gifford organization), had requested the Friends Service Committee to go into the bituminous mining communities in West Virginia and Kentucky to take care of the

* Sub-committee of the Committee on Manufactures considering the LaFollette-Costigan Bill.

starving children. Mr. Pickett testified that the area of need in these mining districts was so great "that we drew an arbitrary line to hit the worst spots first." He added:

"Now we are studying each community, so that we probably will have to include a good many more, because we are putting our feeding on the basis of the weight of the child, and also certain other factors which we discover by a case study of families. *The first thing we do is to weigh all the children in the school, and automatically put on the list to be fed all who are 10 per cent underweight.*"

"In these surveys of the schools," Senator La Follette asked, "what percentage of the school children did you find underweight?"

"It ranges from 20 to 90 per cent," Mr. Pickett answered. "We found in one school of 100 children that 99 were underweight. That is the worst we have found. We have found a good many that were 85 to 90 per cent, and then ranging down as low as 20."

"Are the children retarded in their physical development?" Senator Costigan asked.

"I do not think you would find many cases of seriously retarded physical development," Mr. Pickett answered. "We find drowsiness, lethargy, and sleepiness."

"A mental retardation?"

"A mental retardation, but not often physical retardation."

Mr. Pickett also stated that in the mining areas of West Virginia and Kentucky the relief work done by the counties was not adequate because of reduced tax values and the large amount of uncollectible taxes, as well as the large number of bank failures. Little was being done to feed adults.

The White House issued telegrams and letters from governors of some other states endorsing President Hoover's attitude. Among them were the following resounding platitudes: "Rhode Island is not unmindful of the heritage of self-reliance and of courage and of thrift bequeathed by the founders." "I think I am speaking for a great majority of the people of the State of Vermont when I say to you that the people of Vermont are for a government supported by the people rather than a people supported by the government." "We Hoosiers stand unalterably opposed to the false doctrine of federal patriotism or 'dole' system and feel that financial aid from the Federal Government not only is unnecessary but undesirable."

That local relief was entirely inadequate to take care of the millions of unemployed and their dependents in the winter of 1931–1932 was obvious to those in the local communities who had to cope with the severe problem. It was also obvious to the governors of most of the states, but the national administration still clung to its shibboleth that local relief was the only legitimate form of relief, and that the problem was being met adequately by municipal, county and state efforts. Gifford Pinchot, Governor of Pennsylvania, wrote an article on "The Inadequacy of Local Relief," which was published in the *Survey Graphic* for January, 1932. In the course of his article Governor Pinchot said:

"Our methods so far have been restricted substantially to local relief. Those in high places have continually insisted that a national emergency be met with local aid alone. They have left it all, with the exception of a bit of benevolent advertising, to the states and communities themselves. To requests and plans for federal aid they have cried 'dole, dole.'

Why aid given by a nation should be a dole, and precisely the same aid given by a state or a city should not be a dole, I have never been able to understand . . .

"Where does the bulk of local relief come from? Who carries the load? It comes from and is carried by those who pay taxes to the municipal and county and sometimes to state governments. The Russell Sage Foundation, reporting for eighty-one cities, found that in past years private funds supplied only 28 per cent of the relief. Tax funds supplied the other 72 per cent. In some cities over 90 per cent came from tax funds.

"How are these taxes raised? The answer is that municipalities raise their funds mainly through real estate and other property taxes. Local relief of this kind means an increase in property taxes. This increase in property taxes and the sort of enforced charity by which industry takes a day's pay out of every twenty or so in the month from workers, even from scrubwomen in offices, to help swell relief funds—that is how the program of local relief works out. Yet it is substantially true that every cent a man of small means contributes to relief either directly or indirectly through increased taxes is taken out of consumption. His buying power is slowed down by exactly that much. And the slowing down of buying power means the slowing down of the wheels of industry. Here, then, is the heart of the local-relief plan. By cutting down consuming power, it can only serve to further our economic maladjustment and to sink us deeper in the hole. . . .

"Before going further let us see what sort of an economic structure these men have been building— these men who have consistently opposed the idea of federal relief. By the steady drying up of the springs of purchasing power and the overstimulation of production, there has been developed in this country the most astounding concentration of wealth in the hands of a few men that the world has ever known. Here is the basic evil which has brought on the depression, and which we must guard against in planning relief for the future. Here is the evil which is protected and fostered by local-relief plans.

"You may ask how federal-relief funds can be used. In two ways. First by supplementing the efforts of the states, cities and other municipal organizations for feeding and otherwise helping people who cannot get work. Second, to give work. There is scarcely any limit to the number of men who could be employed by the federal government in great public works of many kinds in every part of the country. Flood control on the Mississippi and other rivers, the development of inland waterways, reforestation and fire prevention, the use of rivers for water supply, irrigation and power, the checking of erosion, the construction of airports and the lighting of airways, the drainage of swamp land, the building of highways—all these and many others can be undertaken and will pay for themselves over and over again in the recreated efficiency of national life. More than twenty-four hundred years before the Christian era the rulers of Egypt were faced with the question of employing idle labor. It was answered by the most widespread and effective public-construction program the world up to that time had known. The Nile was harnessed. Irrigation lakes and canals, public buildings and monuments, entire cities, were built on a nationwide scale. Are we lacking in the vision and the courage that set a nation at work forty-three centuries ago?

"The picture is now complete. Local relief means making the poor man pay. Local relief serves to weaken further our national consuming power and block any hope of permanent recovery. Local relief is part of a vicious policy to shield concentrated wealth—a policy which brought on the depression and has kept it with us for two long years. Local relief means release for the rich, not relief for the poor. . . ."

Testifying at the hearings on the La Follette-Costigan Bill providing for Federal relief appropriations in December, 1931, Governor Pinchot stated that when he asked for Federal aid for Pennsylvania in August, 1931, he was told by some administration followers that he was disgracing the state. Governor Pinchot quoted the statement of Senator Reed, of Pennsylvania, who said on August 20, 1931:

"Finding work for people who need it is a local problem. Our neighbors who want work are entitled to our help, not as a charity but in common justice. We cannot shove the responsibility on to President Hoover. It seems to me that the very self-respect of the individual States is at stake. We must face our own problem, tackle our own task, care for our own people, and leave Washington to cope with the work that properly belongs to it."

Commenting on this statement, Governor Pinchot told the La Follette-Costigan committee: "I want to contrast that with the action of the machine to which Senator Reed belongs in defeating substantially the whole program for relief in Pennsylvania, and, so far as Pittsburgh is concerned, not even raising the quota originally set."

The slogans of the Woods Committee in 1930–1931 had been "Give a Job" and "Spruce Up."

"Spread the Work," became one of the leading slogans of the Gifford organization in 1931–1932. Writing to Walter S. Gifford on November 11, 1931, Dr. R. A. Stevenson, director of the Employment Stabilization Research Institute of the University of Minnesota, pointed out the evils of the spread-the-work idea. He wrote:

"What this appears to mean is a request on the part of industry asking American Labor to bear the major cost of unemployment relief. If industry in a community requires employment of say 100,000 workers in normal times and only 75,000 workers in a period of depression, then to spread that work over the whole 100,000 means to me that we are asking 75,000 workers to bear the cost of the support for 25,000. . . . If we have a job that takes six days a week of work and ask the employer to spread the work to two operatives, each obtaining three days' work a week, we are indirectly forcing one of these operatives to contribute fifty per cent of his income to unemployment relief. So far as I am able to determine, no such request has been made of those in managerial positions or of capital. This large contribution on the part of workers is entirely out of proportion to their responsibilities in the present emergency. . . . Certainly labor is going to raise the very pertinent question as to why it should be assessed fifty to seventy-five per cent of its income for relief at a time when others are talking in terms of from one to five per cent. I fear that if a constructive program is not proposed whereby those rendered idle by the lessening of industrial output are supported from some other source than their fellow workers, we may expect to experience some disorders of a more serious nature than we have seen so far."

Replying to this letter on November 20, 1931, Harry A. Wheeler, chairman of the Committee on Employment Plans and Suggestions of the Gifford organization, stated:

"I believe you will also concede that no employee under our present system has a mortgage on a six-day job. If his employer asks him to share that job for part time he has not taken away from the employee laid off something that is his inalienable right."

On December 16, 1931, the Committee on Public Works of the President's Organization on Unemployment Relief sent a long report to Mr. Gifford. Five major suggestions had been presented to this committee of the Gifford organization, which was headed by James R. Garfield. The suggestions called for acceleration of Federal projects already authorized by Congress under the Federal ten-year program of public works; congressional appropriations for projects already authorized but for which funds had not yet been made available and appropriations for new projects recommended by departments of the government but not yet acted upon by Congress; appropriations by Congress of large sums to be given or loaned to the states and municipalities for public works to be constructed by the states and the municipalities; additional Federal road appropriations; and the floating of Federal bond issues to raise five billion dollars for public works.

The committee of the Gifford organization evinced negative reactions to all of these suggestions. In its opinion, the Federal ten-year program of normal public building had been expedited as much as possible. There had been complaints previously to both the Woods Committee and the Gifford organization that the ordinary Federal projects for public buildings had been seriously delayed by the Treasury Department. The Committee on Public Works felt that additional public building projects could not be made available fast enough to supply important employment during the winter of 1931–1932. It felt the same about additional appropriations by Congress for projects approved but not yet appropriated for. The committee's report remarked that the Federal Employment Stabilization Board, created by Congress on February 10, 1931, was proving very useful as a means for developing a long-range Federal public works program, enabling the government to plan for years in advance, and coordinating the entire Federal building program. The committee did not seem to realize that the United States was confronted with a crisis, and that it did not have quiet years to plan but millions of destitute to employ. The report stated: "The committee believes that continuous progress toward such a goal should not be disrupted by immediate appropriations in the hope of meeting an emergency."

The Garfield committee was also of the opinion that large appropriations by Congress to be loaned or given to the states and municipalities "are unsound in principle." First of all, the committee maintained, it had never been done before. Secondly, it would lead to ever-increasing demands, and "would necessarily weaken the sense of responsibility of the municipalities and states to provide for their local needs and welfare, and would postpone, if not prevent, the adoption by the localities of wise, local, long-time construction plans." Again the committee was so concerned about the far future that it forgot the immediate need. The report also doubted whether sufficient numbers of unemployed workers could be found in some parts of the country to carry on a large public works program. "The advocates of vast appropriations for public works as a means of relieving unemployment during the present winter," the committee reported, "seem to assume that labor can be shifted readily from its normal work to emergency construction, or moved from home surroundings to new localities." This should not be done, the committee felt.

"Unemployment should be met by private resources marshalled locally to grapple with a problem predominantly local in character," the committee insisted. "In the long run the real problem of unemployment must be met by private business initiative if it is to be permanent." In the meantime the committee had no recommendations concerning what was to be done with the millions of the unemployed, except that it was the duty of their local communities to take care of them out of hopelessly depleted tax resources. "The problem of unemployment can not be solved by any magic of appropriations from the public treasury," the committee continued. President Hoover had told Congress the same thing in December, 1930. "Under our political system," the committee's report continued, "government is not nor should it be the general employer of labor. There are times when private enterprise fails: in such periods society must assume the care of those who are unable to help themselves and their children: the primary obligation is upon the local political division where such conditions exist. The response of our great and small cities to meet such conditions shows that our citizens will not shirk their obligations. If some localities are unable to carry their burden, then the states will do their share."

The committee ignored the impelling fact that thousands of men and women were questioning the value of a political system which did not take care of its unemployed when industry could not do so. The members of the committee and the leaders of the Hoover administration adopted a strict construction of the word "society." In their minds it seemed to exclude entirely the Federal organization of society, stopping short at the states. The prevalent opinion in governmental circles at the time was that the Federal government should not take the final step and grant Federal aid, even providing the states were no longer capable of dealing with the problem.

On the question of further appropriations for highways, the committee felt that they were quite high enough already at $125,000,000 per annum. The report then went on to adopt President Hoover's thesis that since the depression was world-wide in extent, it could only be remedied by international economic readjustments. Meanwhile, the committee felt, nothing much could be accomplished by a large national public works program. It admitted that some stimulation might result to the building industries and to those industries supplying construction materials; it also admitted that such a program might result in some additional freight for the railroads, but the committee maintained that a work program could do little to stimulate other industries on which large groups of the population were dependent. A work program would not, the committee felt, help much in the automobile industry, agriculture, mining "or most forms of manufacturing." "Unless the public expenditures were very large indeed they would not lift the volumes of work for even the construction industry back to the levels of recent normal years," the report stated. In short, because a public works program undertaken by the Federal government might not cure all unemployment, the committee seemed to feel that there was no use undertaking one, so that even part of the problem might be met by such means.

The Garfield committee also maintained that bonds for several billion dollars could not be sold unless they carried very high yields, and the committee felt that if the bonds carried high interest rates, they would cause serious declines in the market for outstanding government bonds bearing lower rates of interest. Thus they would cause bank failures because of the losses banks would suffer in the value of government bonds they were already carrying. Such an issue of bonds would also lower the market for corporation securities and for municipal securities, and that would force business and the local communities to pay high rates of interest for money, creating a serious handicap to business recovery. The committee even questioned whether government bonds would find much of a market at all, maintaining, "This is not a period in which funds are seeking investment." They recognized that there were widely divergent opinions as to the causes of the depression, and then added: "Whatever may have been the causes of the present condition, the common-sense remedy is to stop borrowing, except to meet unavoidable deficits, balance our budgets and live within our income."

Opposed to Federal relief and a Federal public works program, the Gifford organization confined its activities to propaganda to induce the states and the local communities in the states to care for their unemployed.

During the period of October 19th to November 25th the Committee on Mobilization of Relief Resources, headed by Owen D. Young, for the President's Organization on Unemployment Relief, carried on its national drive for local contributions to community chest funds and other private charitable organizations. Radio broadcasts were held, full-page advertisements were published in the newspapers, leading periodicals were supplied with advertisements and publicity. Thirty-five thousand billboards in 17,500 cities and towns throughout the country displayed a poster entitled "Of Course We Can Do It." The motion picture theatres of the country were induced to give benefit performances, the gross receipts of which were turned over to local welfare and relief committees. In 131 colleges and in other schools football games were organized, and the proceeds were donated to local unemployment relief funds. The entire propaganda structure was set up with the intention of organizing local relief drives on much the same basis as the war fund drives were organized, although the sums of money involved were much smaller. By this means it was hoped that individuals who still had money could be induced by advertising methods to part with it, and employees who were still employed were induced by pressure tactics to devote part of their reduced earnings to the relief of the unemployed. The results of these methods proved, however, to be merely temporary palliatives, and while they were being carried on, unemployment continued steadily to rise, until at the end of the year 1931 the number of the unemployed had reached 10,614,000, according to the estimates of Robert R. Nathan.

Will Rogers, speaking over the radio for the Gifford organization, in November, 1931, said:

"Mr. Owen D. Young and Mr. Gifford asked me to annoy on this program. You just heard Mr. Gifford, the biggest hello man in the world, a very fine high caliber man, but what a job he has got! Mr. Hoover just told him, 'Gifford, I have a remarkable job for you; you are to feed the several million unemployed.'

" 'With what?' says Gifford.

" 'That's what makes the job remarkable. If you had something to do it with, it wouldn't be remarkable.' "

Mr. Gifford himself testified concerning the work of his organization before the committee holding hearings on the La Follette-Costigan Bill, which called for large appropriations for public works and direct Federal aid to the states. Mr. Gifford told the committee of the Senate that his organization had formed committees and sub-committees to concern themselves with the raising of private funds for relief, the raising of public funds in the states and municipalities, the administration of those funds, and the problem of increasing employment by the "spread-the-work" system. Mr. Gifford stated:

"The central organization in Washington—my organization—was not to do anything other than to encourage the States to do the work; in other words, the responsibility was to be left squarely with the States, counties and communities."

Mr. Gifford admitted that he had made no effort to estimate the need for unemployment relief with any degree of accuracy. In answer to a question by Senator La Follette on this point, he said; "Well, I will not say I did not make any estimate for my own interest and amusement. I did make rough figures, but I do not know whether they are right or wrong, and I do not believe anybody else would know." He then gave it as his opinion that the best way to arrive at an estimate of unemployment needs was to take the census figures showing the amount of expenditures for relief during the first three months of 1931 as compared with the same three months of 1929.

"It shows the expenditures," Senator La Follette remarked, "but it does not necessarily show the need."

"It shows the amount they have spent at that time," Mr. Gifford said. "You mean they may have needed more than they spent?"

"Precisely," said Senator La Follette.

Mr. Gifford, after further questioning on the same point, said: "I think, by and large, the money spent is the money needed. I think that is the over-all picture. In my judgment, that is so."

Previously Mr. Gifford stated to the committee: "I think what we need is that everybody go back to work and have full pay for all jobs." When Senator La Follette asked, "Do you feel that the problem of unemployment relief is now being adequately met?" Mr. Gifford read a short statement:

> "It so happens I just made a check within two or three days of the situation by telephone, with each State representative in order to be as up to date as possible.
>
> "A check of the unemployment-relief situation by States which I have just made, emphasizes again the existence in some parts of the country of great hardships resulting from unemployment. At the same time it indicates that, subject to action by legislatures in possibly some four or five instances, each State

will care for its own who must have help this winter. . . .

"These private and public funds, however, do not include what is called 'invisible' relief. I refer to the cash aid and the board and lodging extended to relatives, friends, and neighbors; to the aid, voluntary or involuntary remission of debts by merchants, landlords, and others; and to the aid—quite real in this depression—extended by business concerns to former employees. These are only a few of the items, but it seems clear that if the total of this invisible relief, which is obviously incalculable, were known it would be found that the private contributions very greatly exceed the public."

The testimony of representatives of social work organizations before the same committee revealed overwhelmingly that each state was not able to take care of its own adequately, and had not done so during the winter of 1931, to which Mr. Gifford referred. Other witnesses, including social workers and municipal officials, testified that the landlords, the victims of "invisible" relief methods, were at the end of their own resources and were going on relief themselves, that relatives and friends granting "invisible" relief were cracking under the strain, that families were being broken up, and that the condition of the unemployed was the worst it had ever been and was rapidly growing even more desperate.

Samuel A. Goldsmith, executive director of the Jewish charities of Chicago, testified that in the City of Chicago there had been 168,000 people unemployed in April, 1930, and that in October, 1931, there were 624,-000 people unemployed. In the entire State of Illinois there were about 1,100,000 persons unemployed, he estimated, by October, 1931. "In terms of loss of wages, in the City of Chicago, this problem amounts, conservatively estimated, to a loss of $2,000,000 a day," he stated. The expenditures for relief in Chicago, Mr. Goldsmith testified, averaged $100,000 a day in December, 1931. He added: "The point that I wish to emphasize and to underscore is that this is a tragedy for the social workers as well as the families, because they are simply sweeping aside the things that they know are decent, things that they know they should and must do because there isn't the money."

Miss Edith Abbott, dean of the School of Social Service Administration of the University of Chicago, later testified that families on relief in Chicago had no money at all "for any of the small emergencies of life." She said that Dr. Anton J. Carlson, head of the Department of Physiology of the University of Chicago, had made a survey in the schools of Chicago during the winters of 1930 and 1931, "and had been scandalized by the undernourished condition of the children."

During 1931 in southern Illinois the Red Cross was able to give families only $1.50 for food for two weeks. At this time the American Friends Service Committee, doing relief work in the bituminous coal mining areas of West Virginia and Kentucky, was compelled because of its limited funds to weigh the children and feed only those who were at least 10 per cent underweight. But in the spring the Quakers had no more money—their funds had been given to them out of a fund left over from the American Relief Administration's funds for feeding starving people in Europe under the direction of Herbert Hoover.

In the same mining areas the children had to be kept

out of school frequently because of the lack of shoes in winter, and Mrs. Helen Glenn Tyson, Secretary of Welfare of the State of Pennsylvania, testified that the teachers from their modest salaries frequently supplied the children with shoes.

Mr. J. Prentice Murphy, executive director of the Children's Bureau and the Seybert Foundation, of Philadelphia, testified to conditions in that city at this same time: "We have unemployment in every third house. It is almost like a visitation of death to the households of the Egyptians at the time of the escape of the Jews from Egypt." Mr. Murphy added:

> "The use of the word 'dole' at the present time follows the American habit of grabbing a slogan. We damn very precious things with illegitimate terms. To use the epithet 'dole' as something to characterize much that is done or can be done in terms of public welfare work is very unfortunate. It is ignorant and unfair.
>
> "Millions of those in need must look to Governmental sources—State or Federal—for the help which is not coming from private sources. They need to be assured that 'somebody cares.' "

A letter from Thad Holt, southern regional adviser for the Woods Committee, stated on February 12, 1931, that in Mississippi "conditions are reported worse than they have been since the days of the Civil War." Idaho had a serious situation due to the vanishing lumber market. The Mayor of Monterey Park, California, estimated on December 1, 1931, that 1,200 transients were crossing the California border every day, and he maintained that this was a national problem requiring Federal aid. Reports from every part of the country emphasized the pitiful conditions among the unemployed, the inadequacy of local and state funds, and the need for Federal aid.

Walter S. Gifford told the La Follette-Costigan committee: "In brief, the principle underlying the relief activities throughout the country has been that first, if possible, the individual community would look after its own. Next, if necessary, the county would help, and then, if the county were unable to meet the needs, the State would help. It would seem that the combined efforts of communities, counties, and States can take care of the situation this winter." Other witnesses maintained that, first, it was impossible for the individual community to look after its own, to say nothing of the hundreds of thousands of transients wandering into individual communities throughout the country. It was necessary for the county to help, but with taxes delinquent, the counties did not have the resources to aid effectively. In many of the states there were constitutional barriers to raising relief loans and levying state income taxes, and while the constitutions could be amended, the process was slow and the unemployed suffered in the meantime. But even where there were no constitutional limitations on their ability to raise money by loans and taxes, in some states resources were insufficient to care for the unemployed. The result was that during the winter of 1931 the unemployed were not adequately cared for according to the unanimous testimony of those actively engaged in relief work. Mr. Gifford was afraid of what would happen if "local responsibility were lessened by Federal aid." He told the La Follette-Costigan committee:

"Should such community and State responsibility be lessened by Federal aid, the sincere and wholehearted efforts of the hundreds of thousands of volunteers engaged both in raising and administering relief funds would doubtless be materially lessened. Individuals would tend to withdraw much of the invisible aid they are now giving; private funds raised by popular subscription would become less; efforts to spread work and provide work that would not be done except for the emergency would be lessened; business organizations would tend to do less for former employees. Communities, counties, and States undoubtedly would appropriate less public moneys. The net result might well be that the unemployed who are in need would be worse instead of better off.

"Also, the effect of Federal aid on Federal Government credit should be considered. If this were adversely affected, the real cure for unemployment, which is obviously the restoration of normal business, would be retarded."

Mr. Gifford added:

"Upon my arrival here, I had a conference with the press and they asked the question then as to what we were going to do with the local communities if those communities and the counties and the States could not handle the situation and I made the statement then that I would cross that bridge when we came to it. Frankly I was of the opinion we would probably come to it. It is only after nearly five months of intensive work on this problem that my sober and considered judgment is that at this stage, at least, of the proceeding, Federal aid would be a disservice to the unemployed, or might be a disservice to the unemployed, and that the situation can be better handled as it is being handled."

Mr. Gifford admitted that he had no figures on the number of persons receiving aid, and he said, "it would

take months to get that information." He said that he
did not know the standards of assistance given to the
unemployed, that they differed in almost every locality,
and added: "I think the standard of aid given in some
cities in the Northeast would be a better standard than
some people in other directions have enjoyed in most
prosperous times."

"You do not think we should be concerned that
people in Philadelphia are not receiving adequate relief?" Senator La Follette asked.

"Of course, we are all concerned, as human beings
on that subject, but whether we should be concerned in the Federal Government officially with it,
unless it is so bad it is obviously scandalous, and
even then we would not be obliged to be concerned.
I think there is a grave danger in taking the determination of these things into the Federal Government. I think the country is built up on a very
different basis. Conditions differ so greatly in the different parts of the country that the idea of trying
to apply one rule would simply result in breaking
the thing down."

"If that be so, why was any national organization
formed?" Senator La Follette asked.

"Principally, I think, to stimulate the local organizations and keep them busy on the problem."

Senator La Follette quoted the testimony of Allen
Burns, head of the community chest movement, that in
cities like Philadelphia, Cleveland and Pittsburgh, and
in most successful community chest cities, "we are just
appalled and absolutely dumbfounded as to how they
are going to get funds to get through." Senator La Follette asked Mr. Gifford if he thought that that was an
alarmist view. Mr. Gifford replied: "They are getting

through today," and he added that it was a city or state problem.

"When you say they are getting through," Senator La Follette asked, "do you think a family of two adults and two dependent children is getting through on $5.50 a week in a city like Philadelphia?"

"If that is the exclusive aid, I would not think so," Mr. Gifford answered.

"You would think it inadequate?"

"I should think so. I would hate to have to see them have to do it, certainly."

"You would not like to try that yourself for your own family?"

"Not very well."

"What do you think would happen to your standards of living and the health conditions of your dependents, if you were forced to exist on $5.50 a week?"

"Obviously they would be very bad."

"Have you noticed the testimony of Miss Kahn, of the Jewish Social Workers in Philadelphia, who said there were hundreds of houses in Philadelphia where families were living in 6-room houses—6 families living in one 6-room house? Do you think that is an adequate meeting of the problem of relief?"

"Six families living in one house?" Mr. Gifford asked.

"In a 6-room house."

"I do not know whether I could answer that without knowing everything about it," Mr. Gifford replied, "because in prosperous times I regret to say, unfortunately, you find conditions like that. Whether we can, as much as we might like to, under these conditions, and in these times, remedy conditions which we could not remedy in more prosperous times, I doubt."

Senator Costigan asked Mr. Gifford:

"May I ask with respect to another question by Senator La Follette which you answered, what evidence of human need in America would be required to satisfy you that the Federal Government should make an appropriation?"

Mr. Gifford answered:

"I think if a State government were absolutely broke and could not raise any more money by taxes or otherwise, that would be pretty satisfactory, assuming now that the local communities and counties could not do the thing directly and State aid was asked and the State legislature met and they could not sell any bonds and the tax limits had been reached and they could not tax anybody. I think that would be pretty good evidence."

CHAPTER III

THE MISERY OF THE NATION

DURING 1931 and 1932 there were continuous attempts on the part of some members of the Senate and the House of Representatives to pass an adequate unemployment relief bill, providing for Federal appropriations to aid the states. The record of legislative action on those bills has for its refrain those sad words for the unemployed, "Died in committee" or "Laid on the table."

Senators La Follette, Costigan and Wagner were leaders in the effort to provide some form of Federal unemployment relief.

On December 14, 1931, Senator Wagner introduced a bill providing for a two billion dollar public works program. The next day Senator Black offered a bill for an issue of one billion dollars in government bonds, the proceeds of which were to be used for public works. Both were ordered to lie on the table. At every session of the 72nd Congress Senators La Follette and Costigan introduced bills providing for unemployment relief and appropriating sums ranging from $375,000,000 to $500,-000,000 for the purpose. They either died in committee or failed to pass, in spite of the fact that the hearings held in connection with them brought out the dreadful conditions of distress prevalent throughout the country and among all classes of the population. Senator Cutting introduced a bill in May, 1932, providing for a five billion dollar public works program, but that, too, died in committee. Meanwhile, Senator Wagner kept introducing his bill for the Reconstruction Finance Corporation to extend to the states grants and loans for unemployment relief, but without effect.

In its continued opposition to the enactment of Federal relief measures, the administration was supported wholeheartedly by the formal representatives of business in the United States. "The Platform of American Industry," drawn up under the auspices of the National Association of Manufacturers in 1932, stated:

> "We oppose the enactment of compulsory laws which give to the individual a right to payments while unemployed from a fund created by legislative order and subject to continuing political pressure for increases without relation to periods of employment and contribution. Experience demonstrates that such public doles tend to continue and exaggerate the evil by subsidizing uneconomic factors in industry."

On February 2, 1932, Silas H. Strawn, president of the Chamber of Commerce of the United States, wrote to Representative Bernhard M. Jacobsen of Iowa, chairman of the Sub-committee on Unemployment Relief of the House Committee on Labor. Mr. Strawn asked that his letter be placed in the record as "the point of view of businessmen's organizations throughout the country," based on the reactions of chambers of commerce and "similarly representative commercial organizations, which are closely informed about conditions in their cities and have an important part in plans for meeting them, particularly in plans for adequate funds." Mr. Strawn added:

"The question about the possibility of conditions being met locally, by those who obviously can best know conditions as they exist, was formally before our organization members in December. In a referendum which closed on December 14, 1931, the question was before them whether or not there should be any federal appropriations for relief. On the ground that needed relief should be provided through private contributions and by state and local governments, 2,534 votes were cast against federal appropriations, and 197 votes in favor."

The Chamber of Commerce of the United States had appointed, Mr. Strawn wrote, "a very representative committee, which had been diligent and earnest in its studies and inquiries through the summer and fall (of 1931)." In its report that committee recommended to the Chamber:

"Needed relief should be provided through private contributions and by state and local governments. There is every evidence that all requirements can in this manner be adequately met. Any proposals for federal appropriations for such purposes should therefore be opposed."

After quoting this statement of the Chamber's attitude, Mr. Strawn wrote to Representative Jacobsen:

"You will observe that the members of our committee and the organizations in our membership are in the position of accepting burdens and undertaking to carry them to a successful conclusion. They are not endeavoring to shift responsibility to others.

"The inclination to shirk responsibility when opportunity is offered is always prevalent in many quarters. Any prospect of federal appropriations for local relief will afford an opportunity to many persons and officials for shifting their own responsibility. Prominence given in Congress at mid-winter to such proposals is therefore most unfortunate. Their tendency is to lessen the funds actually available now to afford needed relief, and the measures themselves will not make good this deficit, being in such form that, even if at once enacted, funds would not reach those in need of relief until spring."

At that time Chicago, where Mr. Strawn lived, owed its school teachers $20,000,000. The city had a strike of taxpayers and was only able to grant meagre relief to its estimated unemployed population of 625,000. The city could not sell its bonds to bankers for funds to pay its civic employees and to give relief to the unemployed.

Three months after Mr. Strawn's letter to Representative Jacobsen the situation in Chicago was so desperate that those who had formerly been opposed to Federal relief, including Mr. Strawn, had come to realize the dangerous situation in their own community. All relief activities were about to be closed down in Chicago for lack of funds, and the leading citizens of the city, including Mr. Strawn, sent the following telegram on June 4, 1932, to Senator Otis F. Glenn of Illinois:

"For many months the Illinois Emergency Relief Commission has been taking care of 111,000 families, or about 600,000 of the destitute. The $10,500,000 fund contributed by the citizens and the $12,500,000 additional, being the proceeds of the State of Illinois notes, in all $23,000,000, are exhausted. Accordingly, the relief stations in Chicago have been notified by the Illinois Emergency Relief Commission that all available funds having been exhausted, the stations must close tomorrow night. The undersigned, representing the business interests in Chicago, are meeting in an effort to raise sufficient funds to temporarily prevent this catastrophe until Federal aid can be made possible. We respectfully request that you make every effort to bring about the immediate passage of legislation authorizing the Reconstruction Finance Corporation to make advances to States for relief purposes, as a separate emergency measure. The money thus advanced to be secured by pledge of the States authorizing such advances to be deducted from Federal aid thereafter made to the several States for highway purposes."

The telegram was signed by Mayor Cermak of Chicago, his corporation counsel, auditor of accounts, and the leading business men and newspaper publishers in Chicago, including Lester Armour, Sewell L. Avery, Colonel Frank Knox, Silas H. Strawn, Philip R. Clarke of the Dawes bank, Melvin A. Traylor, Henry M. Dawes, and the leading executives of the largest industries in Chicago, including the Pullman Company, Colgate-Palmolive Peet Company, Swift & Company, Armour & Company, Wilson & Company, Carson, Pirie & Scott, the Illinois Bell Telephone Company, and more than a dozen others.

Previously, business men and their chambers of commerce had been steadfastly opposed to the efforts of this committee to present an adequate relief bill.

Senator Glenn read this telegram on June 4, 1932, to the sub-committee of the Senate Committee on Manufactures, which was holding its third annual hearings in the attempt to get consideration for the La Follette-Costigan Bill.

"These same gentlemen two or three months ago would have undoubtedly taken another position," Senator Wheeler remarked.

"Let us give them credit for learning," Senator Glenn replied.

"I hope they won't think that any of us who vote for it are socialistic in our attitude," Senator Wheeler said.

"The crisis has been growing all the time," Senator Glenn answered. "Conditions are changing daily, and I do not think it makes much difference what our attitude has been before."

"What we should have done, we should have taken it a long time ago, before we let it get to the critical situation it is in today. That has been our difficulty," Senator Wheeler replied.

The attitude of the administration and Congress, led by the administration, made a vast difference to the well-being of the millions of destitute throughout the country. Men were standing in bread lines for hours in the large cities of the nation, only to find that they had no chance, because the relief funds were exhausted. Men were sleeping in doorways and in fields, and women were trying to find enough flour to make gravy soup, all because of the attitude toward Federal relief of their public servants, backed by unimaginative leaders of business.

After the colloquy between Senator Wheeler and Senator Glenn, Charles B. Stillman, principal of the Burr School of Chicago, told the committee: "I happen to have a school in a very poor district, and I simply cannot face the thought of what that district would be like two weeks after that relief stopped. I doubt very much if it would be safe for us to go through the district to attempt to get to our school building."

In March, 1932, there was a serious riot at Dearborn, Michigan, during which the police hurled tear gas bombs into the crowd of unemployed, and the firemen attempted to pour cold water into the crowd, who were already shivering in a temperature of 15 degrees, according to Rowland Haynes, of the Gifford committee, who made an investigation of the episode. Revolvers were fired by the police, and some of the unemployed were wounded. Hunger marches were organized in various other communities throughout the country during the spring of 1932, as the neglected unemployed became more desperate.

In the course of his persistent attempt to minimize conditions President Hoover told Congress on December 9, 1931:

> "The evidence of the Public Health Service shows an actual decrease of sickness and infant and general mortality below normal years. No greater proof could be adduced that our people have been protected from hunger and cold and that the sense of social responsibility in the Nation has responded to the need of the unfortunate."

This statement caused vigorous protest from the public, from social workers who were in direct touch with conditions and from hospital officials. Jacob Billikopf, executive director of the Federation of Jewish Charities, quoted the President's statement at a hearing on the La Follette-Costigan Bill, and added evidence from the speech of Dr. Appel, Secretary of Public Health of Pennsylvania, before a joint session of the legislature of Pennsylvania, in which he claimed that malnutrition was prevalent among children in the rural sections of that state, that new patients in tuberculosis clinics had nearly doubled since 1929, and that waiting lists at sanatoria were two and a third times their average.

> "In quoting Dr. Appel, the secretary of health for the State of Pennsylvania, I am safe in my generalization that the above statement might have been made by any department of public health in virtually any State in the Union. The facts presented in Pennsylvania are not peculiar to Pennsylvania. No one State or city has today a monopoly on depression."

The United Hospital Fund, of New York City, took issue with Surgeon General Cumming's report to President Hoover on the satisfactory health conditions of the country. A survey the United Hospital Fund made in New York City in 140 hospitals led the management to this conclusion:

> "There has been little doubt in local medical circles concerning the adverse effect of hard times on the public health, but as we deem it of vital importance that the public be not misled by optimistic generalizations, we have made a survey of 140 hospitals in New York City definitely to determine whether hospital cases have increased in the years· since the peak of prosperity out of proportion to the increased population. The figures show that the increase has been abnormal and progressive."

Dr. Haven Emerson, professor of Public Health Practice at Columbia University, pointed out at the La Follette-Costigan hearings:

> "May I say, however, that in indicating rather unusual, or certainly unexpected, excellence of the health of the Nation as a whole, we are dealing with a figure which represents the average of 123,000,000

people, and it must be apparent that an average can not at the same time represent a dominant 80 per cent of the population in excellent health and a 20 per cent or less which may be disadvantaged by the economic condition. . . . The dominant picture of the country's health is determined by the well being of the 80 per cent of people, who, on the whole, have been living a more moderate life than they did in periods of hectic prosperity, and in the same period, a corresponding number of persons have been at so low a margin of living conditions that there is a hazard to health which is not expressed in the average or national death rates."

Senator La Follette asked Dr. Emerson:

"Is it true that undernourishment, so far as children are concerned, is not likely to show itself immediately?"

"Children who are undernourished," Dr. Emerson replied, "are more likely to develop tuberculosis and physical disabilities when faced with the exposures in an adult life or in occupation, and we look to the age of childhood to give us the first evidences of deterioration in human resistance and human vigor. Up to the present time those evidences are extremely difficult to obtain, even if they have occurred."

Dr. Emerson testified that the records of the Association for Improving the Condition of the Poor in New York City showed "that there is among the children of the unemployed, i. e., continuously unemployed, a deterioration in their weight and growth, although this does not yet express itself in an increase of disease or in the death rates." Dr. Emerson also testified that according to evidence offered by Dr. Wynne, Health Commissioner of New York City, from reports of physicians examining children in the public schools, "there has appeared to be an increase of malnutrition." Dr. Emerson added: "This is not of itself a necessary proof that those children will suffer from ill health in the future, but it makes us take notice that we are reaching the margin of safety. We have perhaps overstepped the margin of safety in reducing the food supply for some of the children of the unemployed."

Jacob Billikopf, testifying in December, 1931, said:

"Now, I am not an authority on health; but it seems to me, as one who is dealing day after day with the underprivileged, both in the field of philanthropy and applied economics, that where a family is granted so woefully inadequate an allowance as $5 per week in Philadelphia, or $5 a month in Altoona, and where, as in the distressed mining districts, even $5 a month would seem to be a generous sum, it would seem, in the light of these facts, that it does not require very much imagination to trace the correlation between that type of allowance and underfeeding, undernourishment, and all of the concomitant diseases to which the body and mind are likely to be subjected."

Mr. Billikopf added:

"This is what the prophet, Isaiah, said:
" 'And it shall come to pass that when man is hungry he shall fret himself, and when he frets himself he shall curse his king and his God.' "

The thousands of men on bread lines in large cities, the thousands of destitute transients pouring into Arizona, New Mexico, California and Florida in the effort to obtain work and avoid hard winter weather, and the thousands of men in villages and rural communities who had no crops and no markets, did not have to be told by statistics of the effect of unemployment on their living and health conditions. Walter West, executive secretary of the American Association of Social Workers, told the La Follette-Costigan committee: "I think the real danger here is that we have begun to talk in figures as we did in the war, when we talked about 2,000,000 men being killed. They really did not seem like men to us, and I do not think it really seems like families to us when we talk about 2,000,000 families now. We do not think of it as men walking the streets day after day, trying to get a job, how he is going to meet his wife that night and meet his children. It is a real problem for each one of them. We deal with them after they have gone through a terrific process by themselves. At the time when they need all that the community could possibly give them, we meet them on a grudging basis, with relief that is pared down, that is withheld on a doctrinaire objection. 'You must not have the Government come in; you must not call on public charity'—that sort of a doctrinaire attitude seems very unjust on the part of a society that has got to depend on the strength and independence and the ingenuity of those people to find their way back to being productive and valuable citizens."

Miss Dorothy Kahn, executive director of the Jewish Welfare Society of Philadelphia, testified before the La Follette-Costigan committee concerning the overcrowded living conditions of families in Philadelphia. She said:

"Only the other day a case came to my attention in which a family of 10 had just moved in with a family of 5 in a 3-room apartment. However shocking that may be to the members of the committee, it is almost an everyday occurrence in our midst. Neighbors do take people in. They sleep on chairs, they sleep on the floor. There are conditions in Philadelphia that beggar description. There is scarcely a day that calls do not come to all of our offices to find somehow a bed or a chair. The demand for boxes on which people can sit or stretch themselves is hardly to be believed."

Miss Kahn also testified that men came constantly to the offices of the Jewish Welfare Society asking for any kind of jobs, not for relief. She told of one man who, when he heard that there were no jobs, said: "Have you anybody you can send around to my family to tell my wife you have no job to give me? Because she doesn't believe that a man who walks the street from morning till night, day after day, actually can't get a job in this town. She thinks I don't want to work."

Karl de Schweinitz, secretary of the Community Council of Philadelphia, testified that children were constantly passed around from neighbor to neighbor. He added: "There is a complete break-up in family life in those instances."

Not only had people reached a limit of endurance in 1932, but industry was at its lowest ebb. On March 12, 1932, the President's Organization on Unemployment Relief wrote to 23,000 industrial companies asking for information concerning their ability to spread work. There were many replies in which the companies pointed out their inability to give employment or even to spread work, because of the impossibility of securing proper and necessary credit from banks. Manufacturers complained that the benefit of the credit extended to the banks by the Reconstruction Finance Corporation was not being passed on to them by the banks.

The banks themselves were closing their doors in most of the smaller communities of the country and in many of the large centers. Some towns were without any banking facilities because of the failures of banks. In March, 1932, Fred C. Croxton of the Gifford committee wrote to Harvey C. Couch, of the RFC, pointing out that in Williamson and Franklin Counties, Illinois, the principal coal mining counties in the state, "more than twenty banks in those Counties closed during the past two years." Mr. Croxton also wrote to Mr. Couch concerning financial conditions in Westport, Clinton County, Pennsylvania, where two banks had failed in January, 1932, carrying down with them the school funds of the county. He added: "Many of the school children are in tatters and without sufficient food, and the teachers, despite the loss of their salary, are endeavoring to help them as much as they can."

The Salvation Army headquarters in New York City wrote to Mr. Croxton on April 21, 1932, pointing out that the frequency of bank failures was making it impossible for the organization to safeguard its relief funds. "In a number of cases," Lieutenant-Colonel Edward B. Underwood, of the Salvation Army, wrote, "just after we had completed our Annual Appeal the funds were put in banks which shortly were closed, with what distress to our own people and those to whom we minister, everything you can imagine." He suggested that Congress should do something to make this money tied up in closed banks available. Mr. Croxton in his reply did not believe "it would be possible

to get assistance from Congress but it might be worth-
while for you to discuss some of the specific cases with
some of the financial agencies of the Government."

By May, 1932, there was great fear of riots and violence in various parts of the country, and particularly
in the coal mining sections of Kentucky. There had
been violence in Harlan, Bell and Knox Counties early
in 1932, and Harry E. Bullock, chairman of the State-
Wide Welfare Committee of Kentucky, wrote to Walter S. Gifford on January 19, 1932, warning him against
the imminent danger of the spread of communism in
the Kentucky mountains. On May 17, 1932, Clarence
E. Pickett, of the American Friends Service Committee, wrote from Kentucky to Fred C. Croxton of the
Gifford organization: "I suppose that the next four to
six weeks will be the severe testing point as to whether
riots are really to break out in this part of the country."
In a report by Homer L. Morris on conditions in Kentucky, which Mr. Pickett enclosed in his letter, it was
stated that all Red Cross and local relief in both Harlan
and Bell Counties would cease after May 21, 1932, the
funds for them having been exhausted. Mr. Morris
predicted food demonstrations and violence. He added:

> "I had lunch on Wednesday with Rev. Doak, Mr.
> Williams and Mr. Nicholson in Middleton. They
> were all very much concerned over the situation and
> feel that they will have trouble there before many
> weeks and the thought of what may happen next
> winter fills them with horror. . . .
> "Mrs. Hibbler reports that the crowds have be-
> come so aggressive at Hazard at the Red Cross ware-
> house during the past three weeks that they could
> not be controlled by the police and they simply had
> to let them come in to the warehouse and help them-

selves until the food was all gone. They have adopted the policy now of taking the food to the camps to prevent the gathering of such large crowds."

In June, 1932, the Senate Committee on Banking and Currency held hearings on bills providing for the granting of relief to the states through the agency of the Reconstruction Finance Corporation. The Secretary of the Treasury, Ogden L. Mills, appeared before the committee and expressed himself as emphatically in favor of lending money in larger amounts to private corporations, who would then use it for the development of industry and presumably give employment. The Secretary told the committee:

> "There is nothing the matter with the United States except that it has the worst case of 'nerves' in history; and therefore it is necessary for the time being to provide Government credit indirectly so that people will do the things they would normally do if they were not beset with fear.
> "There are two things we need right now: First, to restore confidence, and, secondly, to restore credit so that credit will be available for projects that would normally be carried out. We need confidence and then cheap money for a long period of time. But when you attempt to bust this depression with a $300,000,000 appropriation for public works it is just like asking a 10-year-old boy to go and pick up the Washington Monument and bring it to this room."

The Secretary was expounding the old Hamiltonian theory that so long as the top of the financial structure were taken care of with credit and subsidy, the foundation of our society, the millions of the population, would receive bounteous prosperity as it percolated to them from the profits above. Others, and especially Senator Robert F. Wagner, felt that what the people needed instead of unlimited credit for large industry was immediate jobs for their support. Secretary Mills never seemed to realize that if the $300,000,000 appropriation, which he found so inadequate for relief, was not enough, that perhaps $3,000,000,000 might help. The Garner-Rainey Bill was introduced providing for an appropriation of $1,000,000,000 for a public works program. But Secretary Mills felt that even $1,000,000,-000 spent on public works would not put enough men to work.

John P. Hogan, a consulting engineer, testified early in 1933 that a $3,000,000,000 public works program would have employed between 1,500,000 to 2,000,000 workers a year, that to support them in idleness was costing $750,000,000 a year, and that the interest charges on a $3,000,000,000 program were only $150,-000,000 a year. The stimulus of such a program, he felt, would have proved a good investment.

Dr. John A. Ryan, of the Catholic University of Washington, D. C., testified that in June, 1930, he went to President Hoover with a committee to suggest that he recommend to Congress an appropriation of $3,000,-000,000 for a public works program. President Hoover said to that committee: "Gentlemen, you have come sixty days too late. The depression is over."

The bill introduced by Senator Wagner in the Senate was superseded by Representative Rainey's Bill in the House, known as the "Emergency Relief and Construction Act of 1932," was first passed on July 11, 1932. It had been introduced as early as February, 1932. It authorized the Reconstruction Finance Corporation to make available to the states a total of $300,000,000 as advances against their Federal aid road appropriations. The bill was passed in spite of the opposition of the administration by a vote of 215 against 180 in the House, and a vote of 43 against 30 in the Senate. In the House 168 Republicans opposed the bill and 23 Republicans voted in its favor. In the Senate 25 Republicans voted against the bill, and 11 voted in its favor. The bill was passed and was vetoed the same day by the President because he was opposed to Title III, which provided for an expenditure of $322,000,000 by the Federal government for public works. In his veto message President Hoover stated:

"I have expressed myself at various times upon the extreme undesirability of increasing expenditure on nonproductive public works beyond the $500,000,-000 of construction already in the Budget. It is an ultimate burden on the taxpayer. It unbalances the Budget after all our efforts to attain that object."

The President also questioned the effectiveness of this title, on the grounds that technical heads of bureaus had assured him that it would only give employment to 100,000 of the 8,000,000 he admitted were unemployed at the moment. The American Federation of Labor claimed that there were nearer 12,000,000 unemployed. The President also objected to the provisions of the bill granting further expansion of authority to the RFC to make loans to public and private corporations, states and municipalities for self-liquidating public works.

Finally, on July 16, 1932, a bill almost identical with the Wagner-Rainey Act was passed by the House and the Senate, calling for the same amount of funds to be appropriated for relief in the states and was approved by the President on July 21st. In his campaign speech of October 22, 1932, at Detroit, Michigan, President Hoover said:

"Various conferences were carried on in an endeavor to arrive at an adequate relief bill, expanding activities of the Reconstruction Finance Corporation, but the Democratic leaders insisted not upon economy but upon inclusion in it of a new item of $322,-000,000 of further expenditures from the Federal Treasury. Ultimately this bill passed Congress, containing not only these provisions but also measures putting the Government into wholesale pawnbroking with unlimited use of Federal Government credit. On July 11th I vetoed this bill and again protested about the item of $322,000,000 requesting at least that such a reservation be made as would hold back the expenditure until it could be determined if the Budget be balanced. In order to secure the relief bill at all, with these very vital provisions in relief of distress, employment, and agriculture, I was compelled finally to accept it with inadequate safeguards to that $322,-000,000, and this expenditure has been forced upon the Government by the Democratic leaders."

The Emergency Relief and Construction Act of 1932, as finally approved on July 21st, authorized the RFC to make available to the states $300,000,000 to be used in furnishing relief and work relief to needy and distressed people. Not more than 15 per cent of the $300,000,000 was to be available for any one state. The advances to the states were also to bear interest at the rate of 3 per cent per annum, and were to be reimbursed to the Treasury with interest at 3 per cent by making annual deductions, beginning with the fiscal year 1935, from the regular apportionments made by the Federal government for aid of the states and territories in building highways.

The bill required the governors of the states and territories to certify the necessity for funds for relief in their communities, and the governors were responsible for the disbursement of the money. The bill also authorized the RFC to make loans to states, municipalities and political subdivisions of states, as well as public corporations, for the financing of self-liquidating projects authorized under Federal, state or municipal law. The RFC was authorized to purchase securities from the communities for these loans. It also authorized similar loans for housing and slum clearance and loans to private corporations for construction and improvement of bridges, tunnels, docks and other public works. It also authorized the RFC to make loans to finance the sales of agricultural surpluses in foreign markets.

This Emergency Relief and Construction Act of 1932 was the only act carrying provisions for the Federal relief of unemployment ever enacted into law during the Hoover administration. Before it was signed by the President the RFC began to receive urgent applications from the governors of the states for money grants.

In their applications, which were accompanied by certification of the necessity for relief and information concerning that necessity, the governors of the states brought to light material on the prevalent great distress throughout the nation.

Governor Pinchot of Pennsylvania applied for $45,-000,000, the largest amount permissible for any one state to borrow under the law. In his formal application Governor Pinchot stated: "There are more than 1,150,-000 people totally unemployed in Pennsylvania today." He added that Pennsylvania's unemployed had in-

creased by a quarter of a million, or 28 per cent, in the
past eight months from July, 1932, and in that month
amounted to more than 30 per cent of the state's working population. Another 30 per cent of Pennsylvania's
workers, the Governor stated, were employed half
time or less. Only about two-fifths of Pennsylvania's
normal working population held full-time jobs in July,
1932. Governor Pinchot estimated that if $60,000,000
were spent among the unemployed of Pennsylvania, it
would only give each of them 13 cents' worth of food
per day for one year. "The $45,000,000 for which I
apply," the Governor wrote, "would do no more than
keep our destitute citizens on an irreducible minimum
of food alone until April (1933) and no longer." After
some delay the Board of the RFC made available for
Pennsylvania a total of $11,304,448.

Governor Louis L. Emmerson of Illinois had made
application to the RFC for $10,050,000 for three months
for the relief of the 1,150,000 unemployed in Illinois,
the estimate of the unemployed load in that state made
by the Illinois Department of Labor. On July 22, 1932,
Ogden L. Mills, Secretary of the Treasury, appeared
before the Board of the RFC and stated that while the
Act signed the day before by President Hoover, authorizing relief grants to the states by the RFC, required
opportunity for study by the Board, "the situation in
Chicago seemed to present an emergency of such a
character as to require action before the end of the
month in order to avoid the closing of relief stations."
At its meeting of July 27, 1932, the Board approved a
grant of $3,000,000 to the Governor of Illinois. In Au-
gust, Illinois applied for an additional $23,000,000. Fi-
nally, an additional $6,000,000 was made available. Em-
ployees of Cook County, Illinois, had received salary

cuts of 21 per cent, and, as has been said, the City of Chicago owed its school teachers $20,000,000 in back salaries.

The Fayette County Emergency Relief Board of Uniontown, Pennsylvania, wrote to the RFC on September 13, 1932:

"By October first, we will have at least thirty thousand families who do not have enough to eat.

"In the name of humanity, can not something be done for these fine people who have lost their jobs in a sense through no fault of their own?"

In Arkansas in November, 1932, according to a letter from the head of the Bank of Montgomery County of Mount Ida, to Senator Joseph T. Robinson, of that state, the situation was "insufferable." "Approximately 1,500 families are without shoes or clothing and they have not a dollar in money." Conditions among the sharecroppers of that state were critical, and the chairman of the Clay County Relief Committee feared "a serious social and economic disturbance." The state of Arkansas had suffered from flood in 1927, from drought in 1930, and from bank failures during 1930, 1931 and 1932.

Alabama also reported to the RFC that there were serious economic distress and complete exhaustion of state and private funds for relief. Both bankers and social workers wrote in response to inquiries that conditions were worse than they had ever been in the rural areas, and that they expected worse distress than ever during the coming winter.

Pierce Williams, travelling in the West for the RFC, wrote to Fred C. Croxton on August 24, 1932: "This trip impresses on me the immensity and complexity of our relief task. It is rapidly becoming nation-wide, and the rural regions are being drawn in on a large scale."

The Kansas Relief Committee, offering data on the need for relief to the RFC, stated:

> "The mining districts in southeast Kansas have been at a standstill industrially for the past three years. This section is inhabited largely by foreigners and it was only through the heroic efforts that riots and hunger strikes were prevented last year. All of the coal mining counties are now practically bankrupt, and unless outside help is received this year consequences will be serious."

An example of the quality of local relief in Kansas was offered to the Kansas Relief Committee and forwarded by it to the RFC in a letter from the Ottawa Chamber of Commerce, of Ottawa, Kansas, dated October 15, 1932:

> "The family of John Mooney, 321 S. Sycamore St., was quarantined for scarlet fever four weeks and they were furnished with $9.65 worth of groceries, and when released the Welfare Board gave them one five-cent loaf of bread, small sack of stale cookies, (donated by bakery), one pound of sugar, half pound of lard, two pounds of beans, half pound of pork, one bar of soap, and they were notified not to come back before Saturday. Today Mr. Mooney applied again and was given one loaf of bread and a half pound of lard, this with what they got last Wednesday is supposed to last them a week. I believe this is a sample of the relief that is being given to several hundred families.
>
> "The County Commissioners are distressed as their poor fund is $11,000 overdrawn and the Welfare Board is out of funds."

The RFC received reports and applications from almost every other state in the union portraying grave unemployment distress and financial difficulty. These documents came pouring into the offices of the RFC during the fall of 1932 from Maine and Mississippi, from New Hampshire and New Mexico, from large cities and small villages, from farm areas and industrial centers.

Although the RFC grants were a help in some localities, the winter of 1932 was a severe one for the unemployed. According to the estimates of the American Federation of Labor unemployment had increased by February, 1933, to more than 12,000,000, and according to the estimates of Robert R. Nathan, the figure was 14,597,000. Banks were crashing in all parts of the country, and carrying with them the resources of all classes of the population. Relief stations were closing for lack of funds, and men and women who had money were hoarding it or buying canned goods for fear of a complete collapse of our economy.

For three severe winters, 1930, 1931 and 1932, the unemployed of the United States had suffered untold misery. As we have seen, a small part of the misery was portrayed to legislators in the testimony brought out at hearings before congressional committees, and to the executives of the administration in correspondence and reports from governors, mayors, relief committees and their own representatives in the field. During that time the Federal administration clung stubbornly to its harsh principle that relief of unemployment was a local responsibility, and that the government of the United States could give its distressed citizens nothing but information and advice.

On May 12, 1933, two months after his inauguration,

President Franklin D. Roosevelt approved the Federal Emergency Relief Act of 1933, which Congress had passed on May 8th and 9th, 1933, and which appropriated $500,000,000 to aid the states in meeting their immediate relief needs.

CHAPTER IV

EMERGENCY ACTION

WHEN under the Federal Emergency Relief Act of May 12th, the Federal Emergency Relief Administration came into existence on May 22, 1933, it assumed two responsibilities. One of them was financial. Congress had made available to it $500,000,000 to be spent cooperatively with the states in taking care of the unemployed. In the next four years of the Relief Administration, Congress was to increase its trust with larger sums to a total of more than $6,000,000,000 for the relief of unemployment. I believe it can be truthfully said that none of this has ever clung to the hands of any official who has had a part in spending it.

Of this first fund, $250,000,000 was to be made available to states on a matching basis of one to three. For every Federal relief dollar provided, three dollars were to be spent of public money from all sources. The other $250,000,000 was to form a discretionary fund from which sums could be granted to those states whose relief needs were so heavy, or finances so depleted, that they could not meet the matching provisions.

How much a state can afford to appropriate for unemployment relief is never a purely factual matter; it is largely a matter of opinion. Confronted in many states by the reluctance of appropriating bodies, or by constitutional limitations upon the borrowing power, we employed experts in taxation and public finance to advise us as to what we might reasonably expect. Clearly all states and cities cannot contribute equally. Intensity of unemployment varies widely from state to state and region to region. Per capita wealth differs, as do legal restrictions. In the main, our efforts to urge state and local communities to contribute large amounts were successful without our resorting to drastic means. In some instances the effort resulted in a public fight in which we were not always successful. Occasionally states were not willing to act until they were threatened with withdrawal of Federal funds, and then grudgingly. Our dislike of falling back upon this means of pressure was that it victimized not the state official or the members of the legislature, but that the suffering fell full upon the unemployed.

Those states which took advantage of their real or alleged constitutional limitations laid a crushing burden upon their local communities, which raise 85 per cent of their taxes from real estate. For the very reason that such taxation was necessary, real estate was frequently unable to support it. Our experience demonstrates that in joint action between state and local governments the state should use its own taxing power rather than pass this burden along to the small home owner.

Its opponents had held continuously that Federal money would dry up local sources of relief. After more than three years of Federal grants, state and local communities are putting up twice as much money as they did before the FERA came into existence. States and local governments, as well as Washington, have patiently studied means of raising funds. Also, the public has undergone a continuous education. We could wait for these taxing bodies to adjust themselves, especially when their normal finances were frequently in wretched shape, by reason of the discretionary powers given to the administrator of the funds. If Congress had provided a fixed percentage of Federal aid, millions of people would have suffered.

I have said that Congress charged the relief administration with two responsibilities. The second was the care of eighteen million persons. Four million destitute American families looked to us for their very existence.

We can make less cheerful account of the way we have met this second charge upon us. It is curious that among the almost innumerable criticisms we have experienced, the one most truthful allegation is never made except by the families who depend upon us. We have never given adequate relief. We can only say that out of every dollar entrusted to us for the lessening of their distress, the maximum amount humanly possible was put into their hands.

Our immediate task was to set up machinery for this job. Federal participation in emergency relief brought many significant changes in relief practices. In general three governmental groups were involved in the administration of relief: the Federal government, the state governments, and the local governments. The bulk of the work of administering relief rested in the local governments. The investigation of relief clients, the determination of need, the administration of work relief projects, and innumerable activities connected with the disbursement of funds to the people in need were all conducted by local officials of the local relief administrations. Contrary to a popular misconception, the Federal government did not directly administer relief in the localities. Local governments in their relief activities were supervised by the state emergency relief administrations, and in turn the state administrations were subject to a minimum of Federal regulations. These regulations were essential to assure relatively uniform standards and honest administration of the funds. Thus the emergency relief program has been primarily a local relief program, operated by local relief officials, but financed largely by Federal funds. We decided that all sums should be spent only through public agencies. There existed a large army of professional social workers and of public spirited citizens who, as paid or as volunteer workers, had been struggling with this overwhelming burden of dependency before the relief administration opened its doors. We felt that if these persons were to help administer public relief, they should come upon the public payroll and be paid commensurately with other public servants.

Over and above these persons in the states there had to be chosen some outstanding man for state administrator who would have a well-knit organization under him. We have found that long experience at public or social work did not necessarily qualify a man for such untried responsibilities.

From the beginning we strove to make methods of emergency relief differ deeply from practices of local poor relief, which still held a heavy hand over many local agencies. Under the philosophy of this ancient practice, the applicant was in some way morally deficient. He must be made to feel his pauperism. Every help which was given him was to be given in a way to intensify his sense of shame. Usually he was forced to plead his destitution in an offensively dreary room. We asked for the establishment of respectable light quarters conveniently placed in the neighborhoods of those who had to use them. We tried to have the applicant received by an intelligent and sympathetic human being who did not, in his own mind, put a stigma upon the unfortunate person before him. We tried to see that relief officials were people who understood that the predicament of the worker without a job is an economic predicament not of his own making; that his religion, race or party is irrelevant. His need was the only thing that had to be established.

Nevertheless, since it was our duty to see that this money reached those persons for whom it was intended in maximum amounts, we had continuously to investigate families to see that no one obtained relief who could get along without it.

Hence we have to admit that relief investigators have entered the front door of millions of private homes hitherto holding themselves sacred against intrusion, and have pried into painful matters: Have you a mortgage? Have you back taxes? Who is related to whom? How much do you owe the grocer? How much were you able to put in the bank? What do you need in the way of clothes to keep the children warm? What food have you got in the house to put in their stomachs? Have you any coal? These were the questions to which decent citizens, with as much longing for privacy as you or I, have had to submit. Not only persons who applied directly, but those who had been reported to the office although they had steadfastly stayed away, went through the ordeal. It was even a part of the staff's task to report their need to clergymen, to school teachers, to public nurses or to whatever society might possibly assist them. If we had not become so accustomed and, in a sense, so hardened to the fact of poverty, we should even now be astounded at our effrontery.

It is no wonder that when men knew or feared this

was in store for them they kept secret from their wives and families that they had received their dismissal slips. It is no wonder that when resources had been exhausted, the grocer had refused credit and they were about to be put out of their homes, the father and mother went into long consultations as to who should go to the relief office, or that they should sometimes pass its doors two or three days before they finally had the courage to enter.

Probably the worst decisions that we have had to make, and those of the most far-reaching importance, have been those which have determined or affected the adequacy of relief. Each decision had finally to rest with the judgment of a handful of men whose opinion might be no better than that of several others who would have come to a different conclusion. Although for each family it might entail the expense of no more than a few cents, or more than a few dollars, it ran into millions.

Should we pay the rent? There was never a clear-cut decision on this. Sometimes we did and sometimes we did not. For a lack of full acceptance of that responsibility thousands of landlords have taken a loss, and millions of families have seen themselves moved from the hill to the hollow; consecutively from good quarters to bad, from bad into worse.

Should we pay hospital bills? This we decided in the negative and hospitals have been overburdened with the weight of sickness and dependency which fell upon them. We paid for medicine and sometimes for the doctor.

Should we place in institutions those dependents of a family who most obviously belonged there? We decided against this also and families already unsettled with want and strain were further demoralized by the burden.

We made such decisions because the first thing for which our money had to go was food to keep people alive. In more places than could be believed, families had been asked to live on two dollars a month. In spite of the fact that we were able to raise relief from such a sum to at least fifteen dollars, and that we have probably left behind us a basic minimum unprecedented in many communities, we must admit that our prevalent standard had no margin of safety, even after nutrition advisers had educated women as to how to get the maximum nourishment from the food which was allowed them. There have been families who have had less than they wanted to eat and little that they liked.

Light, gas, fuel and water were allowed them; so were necessary household supplies, although we have been told by relief workers that there are homes in America that have been so long without brooms the women no longer consider them a necessity. This demoralization of home standards is an inevitable accompaniment of sub-marginal means of existence.

As to clothing, we were supposed to supply it. Yet whole families of children have been kept out of school for lack of shoes and stockings or winter coats. With increased production of our sewing rooms, where unemployed women have made millions of garments, this lack has been partially filled, yet there are probably thousands of women and girls in this country who have not had a dress of their own choosing in seven years. It is in view of these gross inadequacies of substance that the means of extending relief become so important.

We have given relief in several ways other than full wages for work. At first many state-controlled com-

missaries sprang up, sometimes so large they covered a
city square. They were apt to be centrally located, so
that the applicant for relief had often to travel a great
distance with his basket on his arm, or his little wagon
behind him, to get his weekly supply of what the government either thought was good for him, or could afford to buy for him. This was the man who had, in his
good days, gone into the grocer's, put his dollar on the
counter and taken what he wanted. Now he was up-
braided by the press if he arrived at the doors of the
commissary in a borrowed car or a ramshackle one of
his own. He was considered a public cheat, loving this
form of revelation of his hunger. This is probably, of
all forms of relief, save that of taking over the factories
and having the unemployed produce for themselves,
the cheapest. Curiously enough, it was business men who
recommended it; business men, however, who were not
in the retail business. The small retailers, many of whom
had carried the jobless workers upon their backs and on
their books for years, now saw themselves put out of
business by the commissary. It must be remembered
that at times as high as 15 per cent of our population,
and in some districts 50 per cent, has been upon relief.
Of all forms of relief we have seen undertaken since
the advent of our administration, I believe the commissary to be the most degrading.

A second form of relief, perhaps second in economy,
was the grocery order. Under this system the family
provider was given a pink slip. Upon this was listed the
items which he might demand from the grocer: no hair
cuts, no razors, no tobacco, no pencils or tablets. Often
the grocer, being a kind-hearted man, would surrepti-
tiously swap tobacco for a sack of beans, or take off
a quarter's worth of rice and give back a quarter for

a hair cut. The chief merit of this system, in the eyes of its protagonists, was that the family was forced to get what it needed! If they were given any choice in the matter they might neglect milk for candy.

The third manner of extending relief is the giving of straight cash. This is by all odds the best form of relief except work. Although the amount may be small, it is a man's own business how he spends it. It is a matter of opinion whether more damage is done to the human spirit by a lack of vitamins or complete surrender of choice. Cash relief came to be widely prevalent and the most acceptable form of giving assistance to those who could not be put on work relief. Under all of these systems, the surplus relief commodities, of which I shall speak later, were distributed as supplementary. Partly, perhaps because it was supplementary, it seemed never to have the stigma of charity which most people who receive relief feel so strongly.

Among some very self-reliant people who were never able to overcome their distaste for relief, there arose various cooperative self-help societies which accepted subsidy from the relief administration to be used only for equipment by which they produced many of their own goods. Their heroic struggles to produce something from almost nothing were often surprisingly successful.

During our experience, we have had to make up our minds about several matters, repercussions from which sounded on the outside world. Among these was the decision as to whether we should give relief to strikers. We decided that each striker applying for relief to local relief agencies should have his case treated on its merits as a relief case, wholly apart from any controversy in which he as a wage earner might be involved. We were not in the business of judging labor disputes. There existed state and Federal agencies as well as courts duly qualified as arbiters and adjusters to do that work. Unless the Department of Labor had determined the strike to be unreasonable and unjustified, local relief agencies were authorized to furnish relief to striking wage earners. We have never found that giving relief to strikers has given them an unfair advantage in their controversy.

Records from the first day have been a serious problem. We set up, in Washington, a division of Research, Statistics and Finance empowered to obtain necessary data from the states and to carry forward a research program necessary to forming our administrative policies. Formerly local record keeping, as well as investigations of need in the locality, often rested in the hands of the local overseer of the poor who referred to a list of names in his pocket. Perhaps the barber discussed the needs of his client with his customer and kept the records in pencil on the wall. Almost immediately after the FERA set up in business, the accounting officials had monthly reports coming in from every state giving the amounts spent and the number of families and persons receiving relief. This was no small burden to put upon an already overworked relief investigator who carried the worries of sometimes two hundred families and who had to go up and down stairs in tenement houses or make long trips over the mountains on horseback. In the vast counties of the western states, families might live a distance of several miles from each other. Nevertheless, an adequate reporting system was essential. We obviously could not get maximum use of our money unless we knew precisely how it was being spent.

During these early months, the attitude of the American community was undergoing a deep change. By no means all the comfortable citizens who watched their fellows go hungry had been indifferent to their misery. Frustrated by lack of means of aiding them, they had been forced into helplessness. A new spirit now took hold of them. Capable leaders assumed larger tasks. Men and women who had never been in public work in their lives left homes and offices to help. An entirely new group of public servants were enlisting, were being drafted, and being trained. A new standard of public decency was being set.

CHAPTER V

CIVIL WORKS

EVEN in an emergency organization, change of policy or of administrative practice meets with resistance or dismay. Procedural habits are easily set up. Thus, for every new development or program upon which we have embarked, our enemies, and even some of our friends, have called us inconsistent or erratic. These charges were most frequently made before, during and after the Civil Works Administration when change was dramatic and conspicuous.

Our answer, at least among those of us who were responsible for policy, was, "We believe it would be worse to be bound by a hard and fast course suitable for a given situation at a given time, than not to be able to make even difficult shifts when the changed conditions demand them."

For what was happening was a deep shift of public mind. This was the most changing factor, aside from the size of our relief rolls, in all our calculations. The public itself was beginning to realize that we were no longer dealing with emergency unemployment. Just as steadily as it had moved forward into acceptance of public responsibility for those whose livelihoods had stopped, from the days when it was possible for Mr. Nichlos to write Secretary Hurley suggesting that people should not drop cigarette ashes in what they had left on their plates, so that the scraps might be gathered up for the deserving poor, just so steadily had the public moved forward into a widely held belief that work for the jobless was preferable to direct relief.

As a nation we were beginning to acknowledge that our economic distress was no overnight disaster which would recede some fine morning like the waters of a flood. Direct relief might do to tide over a few months or a year, or even longer. But millions had already been out of a job for several years. In addition to want, the unemployed were confronting a still further destructive force, that of worklessness. This feeling became articulate in many quarters, but most particularly among the unemployed themselves. Letters came, delegations arrived, protesting against the indignity of public charity. Men who had never in their lives asked for, or accepted, a cent of alms refused to believe that the situation had gone into permanent reverse. It made no difference to them in what pretty words the unattractive fact of their dependency was dressed. It was charity and they didn't like it. They were accustomed to making a return for their livelihood. It was a habit they liked, and from which they chiefly drew their self-respect. The family of a man working on a Works Progress Administration project looks down its nose at neighbors who take their relief straight. We can talk all we want to about some coming civilization in which work will be outmoded, and in which we shall enjoy a state of being rather than one of action, but contemporary sentiment is still against "a man who gets something for nothing." Those who voluntarily take something for nothing are put in jail. Those who are forced to accept charity, no matter how unwillingly, are first pitied, then disdained.

As we are educated further into the ways and means of social security we should be able to remove this cloud from the man who has no other choice than to be a pensioner. In our own anxiety to achieve a work program I think we as an administration have perhaps overemphasized the undesirability of relief, inasmuch as we have not been able to remove from hundreds of thousands of people the inescapability of accepting it.

The ways of a neighborhood, however, are not the ways of the future, but the ways of the past. Two community forces began to play upon the already self-suspicious man without a job, who had begun to believe he was no good, and about whom his wife and children were beginning to entertain secret doubts. These two forces of opinion were, first the taxpayers and second, the laboring men still employed. From opposite poles of interest and sympathy they converged upon the man without a job to make him feel his worthlessness still further. The very employers who had thought highly enough of workers to use their services for four, eight, twelve or sixteen years, now began to talk of them openly as lazy fellows or spongers, willing to accept the taxpayers' money. The same persons who had once been moved to sympathy by the pitiful predicament of workers whom they had seen dislodged from regular jobs, now began to lump them all into a general category of the undeserving. In some localities, talk was heard of disenfranchisement of people on relief. The volume of unemployment itself should have argued against such a step. An eighth or a tenth of the earning population does not change its character which has been generations in the moulding, or, if such a change actually occurs, we can scarcely charge it up to personal sin. But the longer the relief rolls, the stronger became the conviction of an increasing number that the fault lay in the greediness and the laziness of the individual, who had now found Easy Street.

It goes without saying that much of this condemnation originated in the pocketbook. Federal relief expenditure was growing larger. That fact, however, was overweighed by the natural limit of personal imagination and sympathy. You can pity six men, but you can't keep stirred up over six million.

At the other end of the scale were the workers who still had jobs.

The administration of relief and the researches we have made into standards of living of the American family have uncovered for the public gaze a volume of chronic poverty, unsuspected except by a few students and by those who have always experienced it. We might well ask where these people have been all our lives, if we did not already know the answer. The poorest have in large numbers been kept alive by the slightly less poor. Besides his wife and family, the American worker, more often than not, has had various invisible dependents in the offing with whom he has shared what he had. Add to this the fact that the American working family frequently demands the combined earnings of several earners to keep it solvent, and the situation becomes clear. Long before the worker lost his job, he had been cleaned of his surpluses by those of his friends and family whose unemployment antedated his own. It is our experience that men exhaust private patience and resources before they resort to relief. The ex-worker, therefore, long before he has sold his last belonging and gone on relief, has been forced to repudiate his private share of public dependency by the mere fact that he is no longer a refuge for his relatives. If he is lucky enough to get work again and tediously begin the long job of pulling his immediate family back into comfort and independence, he is not likely to assume the old role of either patron or patriarch. He himself has been subjected to relief; others can take it.

The jobless worker was thus a double threat to the man still working in private business. Besides being a potential drain on his income, he was a rival candidate for his job. The volume of unemployment is merely a statement of how hard it is to remain employed. Most men on relief would exchange their relief status for any job at any price. If they cared to use relief as a subsidy, and were not discovered, they could afford to do the same work as another for smaller wages, and thus as scabs present a threat to unionism.

Even without the pressure for work put upon us by groups of unemployed, the powerful logic of a work program had been clear to us from the first. The falling away of consumption which occurred within every family close upon the discharge of the breadwinner was not immediately visible, except in financial statements of business transacted. Outsiders had little knowledge of how much food was eaten, soap, coal, gas, electricity and telephone service consumed, or of how often garments were mended within the four secretive walls of a house. But the quick contraction of local public funds had had one result which could not be overlooked. School teachers lost their jobs right and left. Rural schools were closing their doors. The American people are great consumers of school services. They could not look lightly upon their stoppage. It might be all right to give groceries or cash relief to an unemployed textile worker, and let his former customer go without sheets. Sheets are private, and it is a matter of taste, and nobody's business whether you use them or not. School attendance, on the other hand, is widely advertised, even upheld by law. To feed the school teacher and dispense with his services was not enough. With more leisure, there was a greater demand for education, both to while away the boredom, and to acquire and improve skills for a constantly more critical labor market. New York with state relief money had initiated schools for the unemployed a year before the advent of FERA, recognizing that food, shelter and clothing were not enough to keep body and soul together.

During 1932 and 1933 a growing number of unemployed teachers applied for relief after their resources had become exhausted. Shortly after the FERA was initiated we attempted to do something for this group of needy teachers. Obviously it was hardly enough to give them direct relief. With thousands of teachers out of work there were, at the same time, hundreds of thousands of men and women in need of educational facilities. We decided to put these unemployed teachers to work teaching those unemployed who wanted instruction. The emergency education program of the latter part of 1933 was not designed to perform the normal educational functions of the public school systems—it was essentially a special type of work relief. The program included general adult education, literacy classes, vocational education, vocational rehabilitation, and nursery school work. Thus the emergency education program was essentially an adult education program, designed primarily to give employment to needy teachers and to provide educational opportunities to those who ordinarily could not obtain them. During the early part of 1934, the period when CWA was in operation, some 33,000 teachers, most of whom would otherwise have been on direct relief, were conducting adult education classes and nursery schools.

In other special fields, too, there had been a steady growth in work projects. Women were making garments for the use of families on relief. Some projects supervised by Federal bureaus were under way. Broadly speaking, however, aside from special programs looking toward the rehabilitation of certain well defined groups, their work was merely an alternative method of extending relief.

I should like to clarify here the difference between work relief and a job on a work program such as CWA and WPA. To the man on relief the difference is very real. On work relief, although he gets the disciplinary rewards of keeping fit, and of making a return for what he gets, his need is still determined by a social worker, and he feels himself to be something of a public ward, with small freedom of choice. When he gets a job on a work program, it is very different. He is paid wages and the social worker drops out of the picture. His wages may not cover much more ground than his former relief budget but they are his to spend as he likes. I am told that all over the country the response was the same when people went off work relief (and we had over 2,000,000 on work relief) and on to Works Progress. The wife of the WPA worker tossed her head and said, "We aren't on relief any more, my husband is working for the Government."

The project itself differs somewhat under these two systems. The work relief project, although it must offer useful work, and a maximum opportunity to the worker to use his special skill, is primarily judged on its merits as a labor absorber. On a long-term, well planned and integrated employment program such as

WPA, where projects must be sponsored by local citizens, and scrutinized by state and Federal officials to see that they meet rigid procedural requirements, the projects are usually work that should be done even if there were no unemployed demanding jobs. It thus has a separate existence of its own. The consumer must want the product before the worker is put on the job.

Although the idea of the government putting men to work at day labor on force account rather than by contract was an old one, having been forwarded by John R. Commons in the *Federationist* as long ago as 1898, its application to the situation current in 1933 was as suddenly conceived as it was put into action and carried through. Re-employment in private industry was not occurring as fast as had been anticipated. The Public Works program which, it was hoped, would prove a considerable stimulus for industry, had of necessity been slow in getting started, and had not produced the expected effect of speedily reducing the relief load. Throughout the country, in all groups, the duration and inclusiveness of unemployment had convinced the public that in one way or another the unemployed must be put to work.

The very character of the workers who by now had been reduced to idleness, whether they were on relief or not, made it easily possible to imagine a stupendous and varied work program which could be prosecuted. Whereas it seems pretty generally accepted that the incidence of unemployment falls first on the least fit, by January, 1933, whole sections of American business had all but closed up shop, leaving brilliant, talented, and able men without a job. Ninety per cent of New York architects alone were unemployed.

The Civil Works Administration was, therefore, created November 9, 1933, by executive order of the President under authority of Title II of the National Industrial Recovery Act. From the first it was intended to be a very short program, carrying over the peak of a critical winter. Its chief, original aim was to put four million needy unemployed to work as speedily as possible and to keep them at work for the winter. The increase of purchasing power was a secondary objective.

One did not have to be on relief to take advantage of the new program. One half, or two million workers, were to be drawn from the needy unemployed who had so far stayed off relief, but whose morale was disintegrating through fear and the gradual inroads of destitution. With a spurt of wages they might catch up their family fortunes in mid-descent, and sufficiently revive their hope and morale so as to be eligible for reemployment at a private job.

As a matter of fact, the rush to get on the CWA payroll was so great that the arrangement of half relief to half non-relief was not strictly adhered to. Many unemployed workers, who had kept themselves off relief perhaps past the point where it was healthy for them to do so, enrolled now, fearing that they would lose out if they did not take the final step. As a consequence, during the period immediately preceding December 1st, relief lists were overloaded. Local offices took as many off the rolls as possible in order to cut down their relief expenditures. After December 1st the National Re-employment Service undertook the task of handling the applicants, and set up some eleven hundred additional offices throughout the country, CWA paying for their upkeep. The Service classified each applying worker according to his qualifications, so that there would be a maximum chance of his being put at the kind of work for which his skill and training fitted him.

Since an administrative set-up which would penetrate over 3,000 counties could follow only upon a large amount of precise planning at headquarters, it was clear from the first that we should have to reach the employment peak by gradual ascent. On the first pay day, November 23, 1933, 814,511 workers received CWA checks. Two weeks later 1,976,625 people were actually at work. By January 18, 1934, the peak was reached, and exceeded the original estimate of four million by 263,644 workers.

The President's executive order of November 9th had allocated $400,000,000 from Public Works Administration funds to the new CWA. An additional $88,960,000 was transferred to CWA from the Federal Emergency Relief appropriation. By Act of Congress, approved by the President on February 15, 1934, a further $345,-000,000 was made available for carrying the program to its conclusion. In all, then, total Federal allocations for the program were $833,960,000.

This sum of money, like all the large figures with which we are accused of dealing so nonchalantly, has meaning only when it is converted into the object for which it was intended. In this instance it was wages.

The quotient we were after in CWA was wages. We also bought other things with our money. Our average ratio for labor to materials was 80–20. The purchase of materials we could also mark up as indirect stimulus to business. But wages were what we were after. Since the CWA received its original funds from appropriations made to the Federal Emergency Administration of Public Works under the NRA, the minimum wage rates and the maximum working hours stipulated by this act necessarily became the CWA schedule.

Under this act, the United States was divided into three zones for hourly rates of pay. For the southern states, the minimum rate for unskilled labor was forty cents an hour, and skilled labor a dollar. In the central states, unskilled labor got forty-five cents and skilled labor $1.10. In the northern states unskilled labor got sixty cents and skilled labor $1.20. If local rates were higher, these higher rates were accepted in lieu of the zone scale of PWA. Road work rates, however, were to follow those of the various State Highway Commissions. For clerical, office, statistical, survey and professional workers, the prevailing wage of the community was paid, but with minimum rates established. Rates for unskilled clerical workers in the South began with twelve dollars a week. Professional workers in the North ranged from twenty-four dollars to forty-five.

In certain rural districts where laborers rarely make enough to live on, this wage was unsettling, and many employers protested against it. We were told that workers were being spoiled. The assertion that workmen can be spoiled by a decent wage is always interesting, though never alarming. That the sum of money which has gone into the home of any family from the United States Treasury through the agencies of relief has ever been large enough to corrupt a man with luxury is hard to believe; although one should agree that the prolonged necessity of accepting it has almost unavoidably deteriorating effects upon its recipients.

For most practical purposes the FERA was temporarily converted into the CWA. The relief staff took on new duties in addition to their old ones, working without thought of themselves, week days and holidays, day and night. New personnel had to be added to handle the sudden volume of business. The percentage of administrative staff to the whole was greater at the beginning and at the end, for planning and winding up were both technical jobs. At no time was this staff expansion disconcerting since the persons who did the work were badly in need of jobs. A corps of regional and district engineers was kept in the field. Likewise the new burdens placed upon the Division of Research, Statistics, and Finance, in Washington, forced the states to take on added staff to cope with them. State relief staffs were doubled and trebled. Every state added a safety division and a claims department. Our safety personnel was a valuable investment for CWA. It established a new record low accident rate for construction work. Many of these workers had been away from the shop, the ditch, or their tools for so many months and even years, that their work habits must have tended to become careless. Therefore we can feel pleased with this substantial contribution to the safety of the American breadwinner and his family, upon whom, in spite of our increasing compensation laws, falls the ultimate burden of injury at work.

Even with such precautions CWA workers suffered accidents. When the Federal government became the employer of over four million CWA workers it insured them under a modification of the Federal Compensation Act of 1916. The following February Congress drastically reduced their protection.

The pay-off was one of our biggest jobs. Even without the work of buying materials and proper accounting, we could never have got checks out to four million workers without the assistance of state relief organizations and the Veterans' Administration. We called on the Veterans' Administration, with the largest disbursing system in the Federal government, to act as disburser for CWA. Their state disburser became the nucleus of a system which within two weeks extended into every county in the United States. What these first pay checks meant to families who had not seen two weeks' wages, some of them in several years, only the families who received them would be able to tell. The effect of their circulation in business was not felt for over a month, which leads us to believe that many of them were spent in the discharge of debts. Nevertheless, there were instances of storekeepers whose stocks were depleted in a day.

Long after the workers of CWA are dead and gone and these hard times forgotten, their effort will be remembered by permanent useful works in every county of every state. People will ride over bridges they made, travel on their highways, attend schools they built, navigate waterways they improved, do their public business in courthouses and state capitols which workers from CWA rescued from disrepair. Constantly expanded and diversified to offer use for the special skills and training of different types of workers, the CWA program finally extended its scope to almost every kind of community activity. We had two hundred thousand CWA projects.

Roads constituted by far the greatest part of the work. Over $300,000,000 were spent chiefly on county secondary roads, to ease the pull of the farmer to market, or his children to school. This money bought approximately 250,000 miles of roads and streets improved or built. Work done on main highways consisted chiefly of straightening curves, putting in culverts, but above all in the repairing, reconditioning and building of bridges. Since the CWA program fell almost exclusively in winter, and a cold winter at that, the execution of much of this road work was very difficult.

Because taxes could not be collected or money borrowed with which to keep them up, most of the public buildings, town, city and state, were as run-down as the poorer private dwellings, whose lack of paint and loosening bricks and boards had made the landscape shabbier every year since 1929. The schools showed most plainly this lack of repair and modernization. Decent sanitary arrangements or water supply were often lacking. Wiring was defective or absent. Desks were rickety, walls blackened with dirt. Some buildings were too far gone for anything but demolition. We tore them down and put new ones in their places, sometimes made of the old materials, plus salvaged paving brick. The CWA workers put 40,000 schools into shape. University buildings and their laboratories were reconditioned.

Our sanitation program was composed of two types. Under the first, a campaign to reduce permanently the infection sources of endemic diseases in many rural districts, hundreds of thousands of acres of malarial land were drained and ditched, millions of rats destroyed, disease-bearing ticks were eradicated. Sewage disposal plants and reservoirs, some of considerable size, were built. More than 12,000,000 feet of sewer pipe were laid or repaired. Under the supervision of the U. S. Public Health Service 150,000 sanitary privies were built in a rural health campaign which had long been considered of extreme importance in the checking of typhoid and dysentery. This was probably the only type of work done on private property, but the owners supplied materials and part of the labor themselves. Rehabilitation and expansion of hospital facilities was a less dramatic part of this health work, yet much of it was done everywhere. In Arizona, CWA workers built a hospital to accommodate 1,000 tuberculosis patients.

We did some work for the publicly-owned utilities. Detroit all but made a new street-car system, relaid tracks, painted and modernized cars. Telephone and telegraph lines were repaired and improved, old traffic light systems were improved, and new ones installed. Power and heating plants were built. Even a high tension line was moved while a road was being reconstructed, an important feat of engineering.

Thanks to CWA, also, during a severe depression year, the United States expanded its recreational resources to an unprecedented extent, adding some 200 swimming pools, over 3,700 playgrounds. After the program was shut down, many CWA workers, anxious to have their children benefit from these places to play, asked permission to finish their jobs without pay. Athletic stadiums, some of them spacious enough to accommodate thousands of spectators, were built, as well as bath-houses, boat-houses, camps, open-air fireplaces, trails and even lakes of considerable size. The forestry program, conducted primarily for another purpose, was closely allied to recreation. Hundreds of miles of fire-lines were cut, brush and dead trees removed. Erosion was partially checked. Old fish hatcheries were expanded, and new ones built; streams and preserves restocked with fish and wild game.

These were some of the tangible products of construction work in which the majority of CWA workers was engaged. We had, however, on our list of employees some 190,000 non-manual and professional workers. The Women's Division, the Emergency Educational Program and our Administration Offices had absorbed some of these before the advent of CWA. Now they began to work under a program known as Civil Works Service, which could profitably use technical people. These non-manual workers were also the ones who made possible many valuable surveys and researches, among them a real property inventory. Archeological and historical projects of excavation, indexing and research were conducted, supervised by highly trained technicians. About 3,000 artists, painters, sculptors, etchers, and mural painters were employed at Public Works of Art. By those well qualified to speak of the importance of their first venture of American government into the patronage of art, it was considered a major movement in the cultural history of the United States and one of which I shall speak later. This program, like almost all others conducted under CWA, was not dropped when the CWA period ended in the spring of 1934.

A true inventory of CWA would not group it into categories. Set up to cover local and unique situations, it had infinite variety. Minor details of the problems or of the inventiveness with which they were dealt adhere to the minds of those widely scattered persons who participated in that winter's program. The whole story of CWA can never be written. It touched actively between twenty and thirty million people who followed its ambitions, successes, failures and gossip with pride and anxiety.

The speed and volume of the work done that winter produced a momentum which jolted the community. I believe CWA will stand out, even when WPA has become past history, like a precocious child in a family of slower-going but more substantial children. For its special quality of having come and gone so quickly, yet having let loose great forces, both economic and spiritual, it shares certain of the memorable qualities of special events. A fraternity grew up among those who had worked in it, like the fraternity of a dramatic recruiting period. WPA exceeds CWA in scope, volume and efficiency. Without what we learned through our CWA experience of procedure, labor problems, supervision, planning and resources of the community, we could never have had WPA, and to that extent it can be looked upon as a preliminary, almost a probationary, period. Nevertheless, its old officers often recall those few months in which the people of the United States were galvanized to an unprecedented task and accomplished it.

American communities had had a taste of what could be accomplished under a government program for the unemployed. The logic was too simple to be overlooked. Once the cover was drawn away from the need, and we no longer talked about merely keeping the idle busy, that need revealed itself to be stupendous. The workers were there, imploring for both work and wages. Private money was standing still because it could not hope for profit, and by its apathy it was paralyzing consumption.

After CWA was over, many of those who denounced it as folly, and loudly complained about the chiselling, graft, and injustice which they saw or thought they saw in its performance, lamented its departure: CWA had brightened the retailers' tills. We had yet to learn that what we are leaving behind always looks good to those who oppose doing much for the man on relief; that upon which we are embarking looks extravagant, dangerous and all wrong. For a while it was a habit to ask about CWA, was it a success or wasn't it a success? In the relief business where our raw material is misery and our finished product nothing more than amelioration, effectiveness has to be measured in less ambitious terms than success. That word applies better to marginal profit, cash or otherwise. Relief deals with human insolvency.

CHAPTER VI

TRANSIENTS

A MAN who, with the depression, found the whole basis of his existence wiped out, did not necessarily look into an empty future with passive resignation. There was still the possibility that over the hill the grass grew greener, opportunity still flourished, and above all, work was still to be done.

Those who went over the hill in search of work were the transients. They were not bums, although in many communities they inherited the opprobrium that attaches to bums. Nor were they hoboes or professional migratory laborers, although circumstances threw them into the same labor reserve. They were industrial workers, artisans, laborers, who, after years of settled life, were forced by necessity to seek employment in new places. They were dispossessed farmers, travelling westward with their families as their fathers had done before them. They were young men who had never had a chance to work, and who could no longer remain in dependence on their burdened parents. They were country people looking for work in the city and city people looking for security in the country. They were negroes, following the usual road of opportunity northward. They were the aged, the tuberculous and the otherwise infirm, moving to the widely touted climes of Florida, California and the Southwest in the hope that a favorable climate would somehow mitigate the rigors of poverty.

Migration of this kind was nothing new in America, but with the depression it assumed a new significance. The same conditions that caused people to leave home made it impossible for them to find a new adjustment elsewhere. Once they were on the way, their situation became more desperate than that of those who remained behind. Not only jobless and penniless, but also homeless and friendless, they were forced to look to strangers for assistance. Already overburdened with the relief problems of their own residents, as well as restrained by law, communities could offer little or no aid to people from without. A bowl of soup grudgingly given, a place to sleep on the jail floor, and an urgent invitation to be out of town in the morning, was about as far as they could customarily go. Even if each community had been able, financially or legally, to take care of these people, it would have feared to make itself a haven for the nation's destitute by offering decent and easily available care.

Even the most insulated could not permanently shut their eyes to the plight of the transient. One of the earliest open sores of the depression, transiency was everywhere deplored, although seldom understood. Feature writers, finding good copy in the hitch-hiker and the jungle dweller, aroused public interest in the subject. Unfortunately this public interest was not always realistic. To the stay-at-home, confronted with unescapable problems of his own, the life of a transient, free from the responsibilities of settled life, frequently appeared at once glamorous and reprehensible. This romantic attitude obscured an understanding of the economic and social problems in which the transient was involved. So long as he was popularly regarded as a cross between a carefree gypsy and a fugitive from justice, a reasonable approach to his quandary was impossible.

However, efforts to get at the true facts of transiency were already being made in 1932. The Children's Bureau sponsored a survey of transient boys under twenty-one years of age. As a result of his experience with the Bonus Army, General Pelham D. Glassford tried to arouse the interest of responsible persons and agencies. The National Social Work Council organized a National Committee on the Care of Transients and Homeless. A few states and localities were beginning to experiment with some other form of transient care than that provided by the jail or the soup kitchen.

Fruit of this growing activity was borne in the introduction into the Senate of S. 5121, "a Bill to Amend the Relief and Construction Act of 1932 by Authorizing Cooperation by the Federal Government with the Several States and Territories in Relieving Distress Among Unemployed Needy Transients." While this bill was never passed, its hearings brought together for the first time the country's best knowledge on the subject. According to testimony, a nation-wide census, sponsored by the National Committee on the Care of Transients and Homeless, had estimated that in January, 1933, approximately 1,500,000 persons were homeless in the United States. Not all of these were as yet on the road, but it was considered that any homeless person was potentially on the go. It is probable that the early figures, being estimates, inclined to exaggeration. Certainly the stories of millions of wandering women and girls were more sensational than accurate. At any rate the largest number of Federal interstate transients receiving assistance on any one census date was 257,790 persons on February 15, 1935.* This included 123,620 individuals in families and 3,857 single women. The rest were single men.

However, this comparatively small number and the fact that it showed little tendency to increase with time, can also be explained in terms of later influences. Federal relief and recovery measures in 1933 and 1934 had a stabilizing effect. The Civilian Conservation Corps gave to restless and discouraged young men, whose only previous recourse had been the road, a chance to help themselves and their families by useful work. General relief brought at least a minimum of security to people who before had had no alternative but to move or starve. CWA gave the renewed hope of a real job to 4,000,000 people and their families. Moreover, the rising national morale stiffened people into facing out the problems at home. There was less need to move on in search of a place in the sun.

With open acceptance in 1933 of the Federal government's responsibility to assist states in providing relief to their destitute unemployed, little opposition was offered to including in the Emergency Relief Appropriation Act of 1933 authority for the FERA to make grants to the states "to aid needy persons who have no legal settlement in any one state or community," an authority which was the beginning of Federal transient relief.

To move into such a program meant to move into uncharted and hazardous territory. No one knew ex-

---

* In addition there were 42,670 persons classified as "State Transients" under care on this date. Therefore the total number of persons receiving care under the Transient Program was 300,-460 persons.

actly how many transients there were. Little experience
was available on methods of assisting them. Even advocates of their cause were confused as to whether transiency should properly be treated as an evil to be sup-
pressed or as a necessary function of our economy to be
rendered as painless as possible. Some favored a unified
nation-wide program run with a strong hand from
Washington; others thought administrative responsibility should rest with the states. The question of
financing had to be settled: Should the Federal government carry the whole cost of transient relief or
should the states contribute? Most ticklish of all was
the matter of definition: Just exactly what, for administrative purposes, was a transient and who should
make the determination?

There were two alternatives in defining a transient:
either to accept definitions fixed in state settlement laws
or to make an arbitrary definition for the country as a
whole. If we had accepted the states' varying definitions of legal settlement, states with laws recognizing
no responsibility for people until they had resided
within their borders as self-supporting citizens for five,
seven, or even ten consecutive years would have received more Federal help than states which took a more
liberal and humane position on settlement. The relief
administration had no desire to prolong the existence
of already archaic settlement laws. We chose to define
as a Federal transient, and therefore a Federal responsibility, any person who had resided less than the twelve
preceding months in the state where he applied for
relief. If he had been in the state more than a year, re-
gardless of his local eligibility for relief, the state and
the general relief funds were charged with his care.

We met a further dilemma. Should the Federal government, having accepted complete financial responsibility for the relief of transients, provide that relief on a comparatively uniform and clearly adequate basis in all parts of the country? This sounds like a simple problem; actually it proved one of the most perplexing in our entire relief program. In a community where single unemployed men who can claim residence are offered only the most miserable flop house care, how can we explain the fact that the Federal government insists that transients be provided at least the minimum of three good meals a day, a decent place to sleep, a little cash and a little clothing? Even more difficult, how explain to the local family, grimly clinging to its vestige of security and respectability with a dollar or two a week from the local relief agency, the fact that over the back fence the family just arrived in town receives perhaps ten dollars a week in addition to much more solicitude from the transient relief bureau than the overworked relief staff could give local families? How prevent, in such a case, the feeling that the Federal government is actually placing a premium on transiency? How prevent an intensification of the traditional local resentment and prejudice against transients?

The alternative would have been from the very beginning to integrate transient relief with local relief, accepting its standards. This was impossible when the transient relief program was started. Those both nationally and locally responsible for its organization felt they were doing a job in behalf of people already the victims of misunderstanding and persecution. They did not want to entrust the responsibility of administering relief for transients to the very localities that had so long misjudged and mistreated them. They were probably right. The transient problem had first to be isolated before it could be approached with understanding. We learned by experience that where a program is federally supported and becomes identified as a Federal program, the Federal government must accept the responsibility for its standards. It cannot afford to stand idly by while the people whose charge it has accepted are exposed to hazards of health and safety.

The first transient relief grant was made to the State of Alabama in September, 1933. By January, 1934, forty states and the District of Columbia had submitted acceptable plans and received Federal funds for transient relief, and approximately three hundred towns and cities were equipped for taking care of them. Furthermore, arrangements had been made with most communities having no special provisions for transients to provide care until applicants could be referred to the nearest transient center.

Certain traditional practices in dealing with transients were rejected. There was to be no passing on of transients from place to place. Families and individuals might be returned to their homes or sent to relatives only with the consent of the authorities in the locality to which they were being sent. These regulations, generally observed, eliminated one of the worst evils of earlier methods, the forced and perpetual wandering of people without residence. Transient families, who came to be a surprisingly large proportion of the total transient load, were generally treated on an individual basis, receiving either in cash or in kind the amount determined by the relief worker to be their budget deficiency. Shelter care for families was taboo.

The lodging house type of care for single men in cities necessarily persisted. It was regarded as cheaper than ordinary poor relief. Communities felt more secure in having the still distrusted transients gathered in one place. In many places there were no other accommodations of any sort for single men. Struggle as they did, however, with decent equipment, recreational facilities, and whitewash, the hard-working transient directors could not make out of these converted warehouses, offices, stores, garages, school houses, or cheap hotels, anything but thinly disguised flop houses.

Moreover, any relief for the unemployed embraced the principle that able-bodied men should work from twenty-four to thirty hours a week at some work of a public character, yet the CWA and the local work programs absorbed most of the local workers. In many rural areas there were good projects which could not be done because of a lack of local labor. Even with the CCC in swing there was no end in sight of work which needed to be done on public forest and park lands. Emergency landing fields, water conservation, soil erosion, fish hatchery, game preserve, pest control, river and stream clearance, and rural road projects could all be undertaken in connection with transient camps. Thus officials began to consider the idea of operating camps, and the character of work for able-bodied single transient men underwent a gradual but definite change. By December, 1934, over two hundred and fifty work camps for transient men were in operation.

Originally, there had been a strong disposition to view the transient as a man requiring "casework techniques" and "therapeutic treatment." But some transients who stubbornly resisted the casework approach to rehabilitation emerged, under the more normal conditions of a work project, from sullen discouragement and inertia into highly effective workmen. There could be little doubt that what most of them needed was not casework, but a job. Excluded by law from the CWA and PWA programs, many were glad to take advantage of the opportunity to earn their board and room and a dollar a week.

The principal shortcoming of this form of relief was that it isolated the transient from the labor market. Hence it was neither surprising nor to be regretted that the more enterprising remained in camp for a short time only and then set forth to try their luck again. It was the men who became so well adjusted to the secure, if limited, life of a transient camp who hoped, like certain soldiers, that the war would never end. As the program developed, it tended to separate this less employable group from the rest, frequently into special camps.

Health is a serious problem of transiency, both to the public and to the man himself. The wanderer is always a potential carrier of disease that may prove a menace to the health of any community he visits. No local medical service is available to him and the very communities which exclude him from their health provisions do so to their own detriment. For this reason special effort was made in the transient program to discover disease and to provide satisfactory arrangements for care and treatment. All transient units had their own infirmaries and many were equipped to handle special types of cases. In the Southwest, mecca of the tuberculous transient, camps were set apart with special facilities for his treatment. One of the most interesting of all transient camp units was directly identified with the treatment of venereal disease. At Hot Springs, Arkansas, the United States Public Health Service had for years operated a free clinic for the medical care of persons accepted as indigent and therefore eligible for the free baths of the National Park Service. Unfortunately the pauperism which made them eligible for treatment was evidence that the persons who flocked there could not maintain themselves while receiving it. Relief was provided to these persons, who would otherwise have remained a constant menace to the health of any community which they visited.

Age interjects a new and special element into the general problem of transient relief. The older transient man, frequently eager for and capable of a good day's work, adjusted himself to the security and routine of the transient camp, particularly the farm camps which served a double purpose in supplying food for other camps and shelters. These were the men who twenty-five and fifty years before were cutting the timber and building the railroads and the factories for an expanding nation.

The restless, maturing boy was another story. He wanted from the world nothing so much as a chance to work, and sometimes found in the transient camps his first opportunity to grapple with the reality of a job. Once his original restlessness and hankering after strange places had dissipated itself, many a boy was relieved to return to his family and the familiar ways of his home community. There were others whose ambitions were not to get a job but to get an education. In several cities special lodges were set aside for boys attending local schools. Some of them, without extra expense to the relief administration, were enabled to attend regular colleges. At Texas Agricultural and Mechanical College a transient camp was set up on the campus where students performed work for the college in payment for their tuition.

In two years transients demonstrated, first, that they

were little different from the rest of the unemployed, and second, that they were good workmen. Gradually as the administration of this program became integrated with the rest of the relief program, our own state and local administrative staffs, as well as many others, became convinced that the effort to protect the transient by separating him from the rest of the workers on relief tended to prolong the discrimination against him. On the other hand, the few people who had most bitterly opposed the program enthusiastically defended it when the responsibility for administration was given squarely over to them.

As the WPA developed it was therefore not only legally but also psychologically possible for the first time to include transients in the regular work activities for the unemployed. This was a real and lasting victory for the transient: to be recognized as being no different from the rest of the unemployed except for the accident of residence.

In organizing the work program a number of the features of the transient camp program were necessarily retained. Transient camps with suitable projects were transferred intact to the work program. A special camp wage was established on a uniform basis for the entire country in order to prevent any temptation for transients to shop around in search of a higher wage. The continuation of camps on this basis was a temporary arrangement. An effort was made to reassign transients to other projects, to let the camps lose their identity as "transient camps," and to encourage the idea that camps, where they still existed, were only an adjunct to a useful project, not a way of life.

Once a program has become established, there is probably no completely painless way to bring it to a close. Transient relief ended because, with the stopping of Federal relief grants to the states, there was no way to continue Federal support on an emergency basis for transients. Able-bodied transients were given jobs on WPA. Those who could not be employed were returned to their place of legal settlement or transferred to the care of the state or locality in which they were then located. Transient camps under WPA came to an end because of a strong conviction that their psychology was not consistent with the aims of the work program. The final victory for the transient is only won when, working side by side with the local man, he is known simply as a good workman worthy of his hire. There are, at the present time, no statistics available to prove how many transients are engaged on the work program; they have lost their identity as transients. This is the ultimate vindication of a group which has suffered the misunderstanding and discrimination of segregation too long.

We shall probably continue to be a highly mobile people. Not only will seasonal demands of many of our industrial and agricultural activities continue to require the services of migratory workers, but changes in production methods and markets will require shifts in the total distribution of our population. People should not be asked to remain in a place that offers them neither work nor security. When such a situation exists their only hope is to move on. For the government to aid them in their search of re-establishment is just as logical as when the government encouraged the settlement of the West by grants of homesteads to hopeful people on the move.

So long as local attitudes and settlement legislation remain as they are, there will be people who will need assistance and who, because they are non-residents, will be unable to get it. If we accept the idea that migration is either necessary or desirable it becomes a government obligation to provide assistance to those who fall by the wayside in the process.

The transient relief program was an emergency program, and many of our ideas have changed since it was organized. Yet it served several purposes. It isolated the problem of transiency and showed it to be a legal problem whose solution must lie in the rewriting of laws that arbitrarily exclude the non-resident from the benefits of protective legislation. Certainly it showed that, resident or non-resident, if their need qualified them, they should be eligible for employment on any Federal work program. No less important, it pulled men and women by the hundreds of thousands from the despair of aimless wandering, misery, and the complete neglect of health, back into self-respect and their place in the world as working people.

CHAPTER VII

THE FARMER ON RELIEF

By midwinter of the first year of FERA the farmer had emerged as a third category of the huge aggregation of persons in distress. His situation was totally different from that of the city wage earner or of the so-called unemployables (the misleading word being used to designate, unfortunately, not only those unable to work, but those who should not, for society's sake, as well as for their own, compete in the labor market; mothers who should be enabled to be home-makers rather than breadwinners, children who should be in school, and workers old enough to have earned retirement).

The majority of city workers live on a cash and carry basis. Their pay envelope is their only link to capital and its products. They don't use what they make; they buy what they use. Thus, although the work relief pay envelope may be an inferior substitute to the private pay envelope, it is inferior only to the extent that it buys less goods. It does not completely disjoin the worker from his usual means of life. His solvency has always begun and ended with cash, usually a week's cash; for the unskilled laborer, too often only cash by the day.

The farmer on relief is in a very different fix. Destitution has stripped him of job and capital at once. The farmer's job does not exist apart from his land, his work animals, his cows, poultry and seed, plow and harrow. His pay envelope comes out of the ground. In the past years his capital has fled in a number of ways, and he has been left impoverished, sometimes starving, within range of plenty.

I do not need to describe here such factors as the forces that were to bring during the depression as many as one million American farm families through insolvency to the relief rolls; the relationship of agricultural prices to those of manufactured goods; the misuse of land; the rise of industrialized agriculture with its absentee ownership; the one cash-crop system; the over-bought farmer, up to his neck in debt for land and machinery; the falling off of the market and, finally, the failure of the banks. These matters have had a generous airing in the last few years.

From their low point in 1932, every indication of rural economic life showed an upward trend. Prices received by farmers for their principal commodities increased almost 70 per cent between 1932 and 1936. The relationship of what they received to what they had to pay for their purchases also improved, although at a slower rate. Income from farm production increased from $5,300,000,000 in 1932 to an estimated $8,000,-000,000 and more in 1935, partly because of payments by the Agricultural Adjustment Administration. Yet in the sixteen months following our relief census in October, 1933, the number of farmers bringing their families onto relief increased by 75 per cent. By February, 1935, 733,000 families were on the rolls.

The paradox of these two trends is not hard to explain. Recovery could not immediately touch those persons whose resources were already exhausted, either those who had been in hopeless distress before the depression or those who lost out after 1929. Men whose farms were gone or who had no means to finance a going farm naturally received benefit neither from

AAA nor from increased prices. Moreover, the relief rolls of October had by no means been an accurate measure of the farmers' need. Thousands did not present themselves until they had been in active want for months. A farmer, like anyone else, does not receive assistance until it is there to be received. Early in the program the farmer had a hard time getting relief. Although the government might be interested in him, local relief was being devised for the needs of the town near which he lived, and it was to this town that he went for relief in the form of cash, commissary, or work on whatever project could take him on. The distance itself was often insurmountable. In many areas relief supplies had to be delivered great distances, on horseback in the mountains, by boat in the bayou country. A further reason for the gained momentum at which they were assigned upon the relief rolls was the fact that when they finally came to the end of their resources, they had fewer of the alternative courses to which the city worker turns when he is faced with dependency. They had no near neighbors, no casual charity, no help from lodge or union, and fewer jobs. Even so, many of the farmers who have sought public assistance during the depression are able to maintain partial independence; are aided one month and not the next. When they can sell a little produce or get an occasional job, they take themselves off relief rolls.

It was not until the spring of 1934 that we were able to cut our problem into three general parts, urban unemployed, rural families, and direct relief for the unemployables, in order to cope appropriately with three different kinds of need. We began at that time a plan of rural rehabilitation which aimed to restore the farmer to independence. It goes without saying that the plan which helps to make further relief unnecessary is the best and cheapest form of relief. The best way to get the farmer off relief was to see that he had the means of raising at least what he needed to eat. The supplementary cash income which he had to have for shoes or doctors or school books or to retain or regain his ownership came second to this. To the farmer without seed or tools, a bridge project in the other end of the county has little relevance at planting time.

The relief farmer and his family were costing the government from ten to thirty dollars a month, although there were states where whole families lived on shamefully smaller amounts. We decided to pick out the man who showed the most promise of being able to make a go of it again, to lend him a little money, to relieve him of the social worker and instead place him in the hands of a rural rehabilitation worker who was in reality a farm agent. To do this work we set up in Washington a Rural Rehabilitation Division which had its counterpart in the state administrations. The states were permitted to charter Rural Rehabilitation Corporations, permanent legal entities to serve as the financial agents of these rural divisions; to hold title to, or lien against, all real property purchased or constructed; to serve as payee and custodian of all notes covering advances to the families with whom they were doing business. They could buy, sell or lease.

The corporation directors were expected to include the State Agricultural Extension Director, and a regional director of the Land Policy Section of the AAA. They also solicited the aid of the home economists. This was to help us as well as the farmers.

The inclusion of men who knew the last technical

breakdown of the farming problem would insure a practical rather than a romantic effort, for it was clear from the first that there was no simple category of the American farmer. His situation was almost, if not quite, as various as that of the wage earner on relief. He was owner, tenant, sharecropper or laborer. Even as laborer he did not always fall into that general description of hired man or farm hand which such a term is apt to bring to mind. The hired man proper was beginning to become extinct. As the farm owner had got further and further into economic straits he was unable to take responsibility for the thirty dollars a month or thereabouts and keep, which used to be the living of the hired man, and employed instead a man only when he had to or could, and gave him a day's pay and a midday meal. The FERA had reason to know this. We were always hearing that the farmer could get no help, that men would not leave relief to take a job at critical farming seasons. It usually turned out that the farm hand was fearful to give up his job on a project for a few, uncertain days of work a month at low pay. In those states where the farm laborer was pushed off the relief rolls from planting to harvest, at the instance of the farmers, he was very frequently put into a situation by which he was lucky if he got eight days of work a month and a noon-day meal. Thus the farm laborer was sometimes a farm laborer and sometimes not. He was a casual town and country man. This still holds true and also includes those other farm wage workers, the family army of crop-followers who down to the smallest children work in the fields, picking onions and lettuce, gathering berries, cultivating beets for anything from eight to fifteen cents an hour, and sometimes running into the forces of the private police if they strike for more.

These people also eke out their sub-standard level of existence by following the canneries when they are through with the fields. These different relationships of the worker to the rural economy had further variations within different farming regions. In the South, where in the last seventy years more than 1,000,000 whites have joined the tenant or the labor class, where tens of thousands of sharecroppers were reduced to the position of stranded populations, the means of taking the farmer off relief were very different from the means which would bring effective assistance to the dry-farmer who could not buy water, or the once prosperous farmer of the corn-hog belt.

In the simplest form the problem was to help a man accustomed to working the ground to find the way to work his ground again: If his land was no good, to put him on good land, and to restore his sterile acres to their proper place in a sensible land utilization program already outlined by experts; to turn it into forest or grass in an effort to prevent erosion, floods and desert; to put it back into swamp for game refuge, or into recreation land. Thus our Rural Rehabilitation Program which concerned the individual and his family, and the Land Program which concerned the land as a national resource, overlapped in purpose and practice. Later they were both transferred to the Rural Resettlement Administration where the improvement of these phases of American life can be better integrated.

Rural rehabilitation as it was developed under the FERA concerned itself with three aims: first, to make the farmer self-supporting where he was; second, to move him off bad land to good; third, to establish stranded industrial groups on the land on a basis which would approach self-sustainment. These stranded groups had been marooned without livelihood by the departure of industries, lumbering, mining and oil, which were never interested in an orderly development of resources which would leave behind them a stabilized population. Rehabilitation in place, as it was called, was the most highly developed of these three procedures. When the program began, because of widespread local reluctance to furnish him with work relief, the farmer at large was getting direct relief. By the end of our fourteen months in the rehabilitation business nearly half, 367,000 to be exact, were being aided, not as relief clients, but as farmers, either on land where they were already, or in its immediate vicinity.

To be eligible for rehabilitation a farmer must first prove himself ineligible for other forms of farm credit. His need being established, if he and his family gave reasonable assurance of being good risks, they were removed from the general relief rolls although he usually had to be given food or cash until his first crops were out of the ground. When necessary, arrangements were made with his creditors for scaling down and postponing his debts until the future was somewhat assured. A plan for getting the family back on its feet was then worked out by the farmer, the farm agent, and the home economics adviser to see that the aid to be advanced was not disproportionate to what the family would be able to reproduce. Sometimes this plan and the subsequent interest in his affairs were of more importance to the discouraged farmer than the cash outlay. (His need though important might be easy to supply.) We had farmers with land, seed and hoe who for lack of a plow planted in unbroken fields. Sometimes it was a lack that could be supplied without money: a work animal could be borrowed, if he had the nerve to ask for it. But the farmer, traditionally individualistic, has become pretty dismal by the time he is on relief. The situation has got ahead of him in more ways than one. On the whole his need is literal and extreme. In states with high standards of living, like Maine, Minnesota, Nebraska or Ohio, families on the land were found in unspeakable poverty, lacking seed to put in the ground, stock or work animals for their farms, or barns to put them in if they had had them. Supposed to be primary producers, they had no food in the house.

Advances were made for capital goods, covered by notes payable to the state Rural Rehabilitation Corporations and secured by a first lien on property or crops. Payments on land were not to exceed thirty-five years, and on livestock not to exceed three. Early payments were frequently in kind: Thousands of cans of fruit and vegetables came back to the relief offices. Later, when rural projects on such related work as erosion control, and repair and construction of farm buildings had been set up to give them supplementary income, and when crops had begun to come in, these payments were made in cash. If his cash crop failed, the farmer on rehabilitation would be partially independent, for he was required to raise enough food to keep his family during the winter, something he was frequently not permitted to do under a sharecropping scheme.

For stranded groups or persons whose experience fitted them to be part-time farmers and part-time industrial workers, we proposed, and in a few instances adopted, the rural industrial community. The shared expense of community costs, the development of cooperative buying and selling in a work center where they could process their goods for market, or make goods for their common use, gave these workers a bulwark against the hazards of private industrial employment, although their community was devised around the accessibility of the private job. Their subsistence activities ranged from small-scale gardening, poultry raising and dairying, up to cooperative farming done by the unemployed of the community. Examples of the purely agricultural community, whose chief reliance is upon the land, are found at Woodlake in Texas, Dyess in Arkansas, Cherry Lake in Florida, Pine Mountain Valley in Georgia, and Matanuska, Alaska. The family unit in these communities ranged in cost from one thousand to five thousand dollars, nearly half this cost being absorbed from funds which would have been extended anyway as relief to the workmen.

Even though it is eminently successful for many families, this form of rehabilitation is of limited usefulness in so large a program. In a problem of staggering bulk it can care for highly selected groups only. Until industry becomes decentralized and orderly through other than the forces which seek to care for the human waste which it sends down the flume, and while American agriculture continues to present such complex maladjustment of human to material resources, such a plan can never offer a large-scale solution. We have as our precedent, however, in almost every state in the Union, farm villages whose inhabitants have almost invariably managed to weather bad times without going on relief.

The resettlement of farmers who were living on submarginal lands was an inextricable part of the land program, for they were being removed from land purchased by the government.

The basic purposes of this program had been formulated for years by land economists and conservation experts. At various times a total of $78,390,000 were allocated to the land program, but after sums had been impounded in January, 1935, for general relief purposes, $28,390,000 were actually available for the work.

Our collaborators in land acquisition were the National Park Service and the office of Indian Affairs of the Department of Interior, the Land Policy Section of the AAA and the Biological Survey of the Department of Agriculture. All these agencies had ideas as to how acquired submarginal land should be used. The Park Service was in the business of proving to the public that recreational grounds could or should be within the reach of everyone. The Indian Office wanted to provide western Indians with larger grazing areas. The Land Policy Section wanted to return land into grass and trees for soil and water conservation. The Biological Survey wanted poor land used for wild life refuges.

If we can say anything good about the drought of the summer of 1934, it is that it, too, was instrumental in arousing the country to the need of a better land utilization program. Culminating several dry years of increasing severity, it did what years of writing and talking by the conservationists had never done—focussed public attention on what was happening to our greatest natural resource. Farmers in addition to fighting a maladjusted market were fighting nature as well, and nature at her ugliest. Heat and dust filled not only the sky but the newspapers and the movies. The East became aware of the West as never before, while meat prices fluctuated, cattle trains bore famished cattle to eastern pasture or to slaughter, and the problem of keeping an entirely new stratum of the population from want introduced the quality of crisis once more into the administering of relief. Expenditures shot up for the summer and winter that followed. Work relief in the more than twenty states designated by the Department of Agriculture as emergency drought areas related itself very largely to the saving and manipulation of water. Meanwhile other agencies of government—the PWA, building large and small dams; the Tennessee Valley Authority, attempting to change the economy of a river basin; the National Resources Board; the Bureau of Erosion Control, fighting rain water run-off through education and assistance of the farmer; the CCC, making fire breaks and otherwise fighting forest-destruction; as well as the Department of Agriculture, watchful in and out of season—were pointing out various aspects of land abuse. It had become clear that the farmer, even if he were aware of his situation, which he frequently was not, was unable to change his situation single-handed. It was a Federal, state and county task. Alone or collectively, the human beings dependent upon poor land were taxed beyond their capacity, a fact made evident in rural slums whose standard of living vied with the worst to be found in city tenement areas. The cost of good schools being prohibitive, their schools were of necessity inadequate. In certain counties of Wisconsin it was estimated that an average of four hundred dollars a year, for every isolated family on submarginal land, would be saved by buying the land and assisting the owner to move to better ground, closer to the center of population.

Usually it was not the spirit of Daniel Boone that had planted the farm family in unrewarding wilderness, whether that wilderness was old and overpopulated by an excessive birth-rate (as occurred in certain sections of the South, where large families were often encouraged in order to have an adequate labor supply in critical seasons), or whether it was in the cutover North, or on abandoned New England farms. Purchases of four million acres of land, since they were made by the FERA, were of necessity directed toward the amelioration of human distress caused by this misuse of land. Other benefits accruing from these purchases were by-products, even though they might be more lasting and thus more important to larger numbers of men than those whose personal economy we were able to improve.

Far from his being unwilling to cooperate with us, as was frequently alleged by those who believe that the poor love their destitution, the farmer was so anxious to get on decent land that it was difficult for us to make selection from the many areas proposed for purchase. Men tramped miles over the hills to request us to include their lands. Letters and petitions from farmers stranded on bad acres form some of the most appealing human documents we have in our files. Those who opposed us, opposed for other reasons. They feared danger to state sovereignty; they feared a diminution of the tax base; they feared any sort of governmental planning. We also experienced the individual antagonism of vested interests.

The farmer on relief should be an anomaly. Perhaps some day he will be, but not for many years. Americans are apt to visualize our typical American farmer as an independent, sagacious character living like a small lord on such acres of apparently perpetual plenty as the traveller may see in New York, Pennsylvania, and Wisconsin. This is the type which persists in popular fiction and pictures. He is the one who comes to the city, who makes himself felt in politics. In sections where the farmer's living is mean, his condition oppressed, it has been mean and oppressed so long that he is taken for part of the landscape. If his lot ever comes to notice, it is dismissed as inevitable. In regions of recurring drought, or in dry-farming areas, where he has to be a gambler, he is supposed to take his losses with his gains, to be stoical or else lighthearted, partly because he was thought to be a fool to try it in the first place. The public does not bear in mind, when it reviews his brief, the presumable fact that he chose this means of earning his living as the lesser of two evils, having been pushed into it by economic forces beyond his understanding, or by public land policies which should have kept him from attempting to beat an unbeatable game.

I believe that until three kinds of education are well under way we shall have a large farm relief problem on our hands, to be taken care of in one way or another for many years—a drain on the public pocketbook, whether that pocketbook is kept in the vest of the county, the state or the Federal government.

The first is an education of the experts who must figure out a workable relationship between the prices of agricultural and manufactured goods, and a workable distribution of population on the land. We cannot expect that in a hurry, although I know that, as in all social progress, the knowledge of experts is already years ahead of our practice.

The second kind of education must be the education of the farmer. In all parts of the country we have college graduates on the land. Agricultural schools, farm granges, county agents and similar educational agencies have modernized farm practices, and have been in part responsible for the fact that often the farm owner is a leading citizen in public life, living at a standard his city brother may well admire. Where such men are found on relief, as in crop failure regions, their rehabilitation is truly but a restoration to that which they knew before. Literal rehabilitation, on the other hand, of the characteristic relief family to what they knew before, would be to restore them to a status more insecure than that which they enjoy, pitiful though that may be, upon relief. Rehabilitation for these people must be conceived more broadly, and can be so conceived and yet fall in the category of relief. Because living standards have purposely been kept so low, human resources in many areas are more of a limiting factor than the availability of material resources. Through willfulness or indifference, education has been kept from hundreds of thousands of these families. It is through lack of education as much as through any other factor that they are unable to make any adjustment to changing conditions, especially since the status to which they were accustomed was so low. A man without enough calcium in his bones, or food under his belt, has more inertia in him than rebellion. When we consider that in the eastern cotton belt one-half of the negro heads of families on relief, and one-fifth of the heads of white families, have had no schooling whatsoever, and that most of the negroes and half of the whites have never gone through the fifth grade; and when we realize affairs are little better in the Appalachians and the Ozarks, we have acknowledged a situation which cannot immediately be mended by some packets of diversified seed, a plow, a hoe and a mule. These people, who have been able to do little more than propagate more hands for less available labor, are ill equipped to migrate to more highly developed labor markets. When they do so, as they have done for instance from Mississippi into Illinois, they carry with them their low standards of life, debilitating that which they touch. Only time can raise them.

The third kind of education which must precede any permanent reduction of open-country relief must be the education of the public. This must consist in relating the relevance of low living standards to the persistence of the need for relief (almost equally true, of course, of the industrial worker, although in the industrial sections law has usually forced his exposure to a few more grades of schooling). A low standard of living wherever it is found produces candidates for the relief rolls, draws on not only the public but the private pocketbook, and undermines the life of the community where it prevails. Because the depression disjoined all kinds of people from their income, we have had many highly privileged men and women from all walks of life become temporarily dependent upon public aid. Every economic cross-section has been represented on the rolls, even to brilliant, erudite and gifted men and women. But the typical individual is never above the line of dependency. Underfed, illiterate and neglected, he never will be. To lift the American standard of living is the task of other agencies than the relief administration. In those instances where in the course of our appointed task we have been able to do so we have, nevertheless, been minding our own business.

CHAPTER VIII

THE FARMERS' SURPLUSES TO MEN IN NEED

ACCORDING to some estimators, the American nation is underfed by some $4,500,000,000 worth of food annually. We have not always known this. Our old time slogans, such as the one about the full dinner pail, bore evidence to our quite general belief that the American standard of living was high. We had reason to be content if we compared ourselves to China, or even to European low-wage nations. The sub-standard areas of American existence had not come to public notice, and probably even students who were conscious of them were not conscious of their prevalence.

It was not knowledge of widespread underconsumption, therefore, but more likely the newspaper instances of starvation and the troubling visibility of bread lines, that created such general shock when the AAA began its pork-reduction program to help the farmer out of the circular cage in which the more he raised to sell below cost, the worse off he became. There are still people who will tell you that all children have all the milk they need, that they don't like it anyway. There are still persons who say that those who don't eat so much are sick less often than those who have a diet of their own choosing. Nevertheless, I believe that the government's planned reduction of food surpluses, more than any other event, turned the critical public

154

eye upon the American standard of living and learned that it was not what it seemed to be. Those who were concerned with giving relief in every corner of the United States needed no such jolt, faced as they were many hours of the day with the painful task of sending people home with less than enough to eat.

The irony was clear, before the event. If there were great food surpluses while people went hungry, the public could rightly be revolted.

To make a connection between the overburdened farmer and the large number of destitute unemployed whose inability to buy their normal requirements had in part created the market surpluses, the Federal Surplus Relief Corporation was chartered October 4, 1934, under the laws of Delaware. The volume of business done by this corporation was never large. In addition to drought livestock we distributed something like $100,000,000 worth of food stuffs in two years: A small wholesale grocery will do a million a year. We distributed around $6,000,000 worth of fuel. The magnitude of the corporation's business would never claim the attention of the success-story reader. What was of interest in the story of the FSRC, now transferred to the executive direction of the AAA where it is known as the Federal Surplus Commodities Corporation, was its technique, and the urgency with which it had to do much of its business. What gives the story its significance is that redivision and subdivision of these comparatively small amounts of food should be of such prime importance to any American family. In the lower levels of American consumption, the discrepancy between a deadly monotonous minimum, or even submarginal diet, and the level to which it can be brought even by the addition of half a dollar, is a discrepancy which thousands of housewives cannot manage to bridge even in good times.

The FSRC was a non-profit corporation with no capital stock, its incorporators being restricted to the persons holding the office of the Secretary of Agriculture, the Federal Emergency Administrator of Public Works and the Federal Emergency Relief Administrator. Its membership was subsequently enlarged to include the director of the Agricultural Adjustment Administration and the Administrator of Farm Credit.

Technically the corporation functioned in a fairly simple way. Through Acts of Congress and income from processing taxes, the AAA had available certain amounts of money which it authorized the corporation to spend for the purchase of specified commodities. Schedules calling for bids were sent out by the procurement division. Based upon quantities purchased, these commodities were pro-rated to the states according to the number on relief. So far as possible, goods were distributed on a month to month basis, partly to maintain an even flow of commodities into the states, but partly because storage and spoilage must be minimized. In five weeks from its charter date, the corporation was doing business. Obviously pork was its first commodity, since pork was in a way the corporation's reason for being. Other commodities followed: butter, cheese, cereal, apples, sugar, syrup, potatoes, flour, coal and blankets. The corporation purchased nearly 120,000 bales of surplus cotton, either in the raw state or as finished yardage, and sent it to state relief workrooms. In addition to commodities for human consumption, more than 13,-240,000 bushels of feed and 16,635,000 pounds of seed were sent to farmers chiefly in the drought-stricken regions for upkeep of stock and for planting.

In the main these commodities came into the hands of the FSRC from three sources: The AAA donated them from the purchases it made in its crop and price adjustment program; the corporation bought outright; and the state relief administrations purchased local crop surpluses. These state purchases were made from farmers direct, first from those farmers who were either in danger of going on relief or already there. One of the largest of these state purchases was of 2,000 carloads of potatoes in Maine. Apples and cabbage were bought in New York, sweet potatoes and cane syrup in the South. In other words, the corporation bought only part of the goods it distributed. Distribution was its first job, and distribution was made into work relief.

The Drought Cattle Program was a severe test of the machinery we had set up for the quick movement of goods from places where they were unwanted to where they would do the most good. When the extent of the drought had made it clear that farmers could no longer keep all their cattle, the Livestock Disposition Committee was formed in June, 1934, to act in all processes subsequent to their donation from the AAA, who by purchase took them off the farmers' hands. Approximately 4,000,000 head of sheep and cattle were condemned and buried, but what was fit for consumption and could not be supported on the range was appraised by a staff of 1,500 veterinarians from the Bureau of Animal Industry, bought for prices stipulated, and either driven or trucked out of the country to a railroad concentration point. Here their title was taken over and their subsequent fate determined by the FSRC.

Transient centers, cooperative groups and farmers on the rehabilitation program were furnished with milch cows and breeding animals. The rest were to be sent to pasture or processed for conversion into food for the needy unemployed. Western farmers, no longer able to stand back and watch their cattle suffer as the watering places and pastures failed them, were in a mood to make this federally-managed retreat into a stampede. The cattle march took on the character of war-time speed. Appraisers worked desperately, while farmers pleaded with them to hurry. Men unrolled their beds in the offices to spend what was left of the night. At times 3,000 cars of cattle a day moved out of St. Paul, in sixty trains of fifty cars apiece.

The saving of the cattle industry was the objective of the AAA purchases of sheep and cattle. Their conversion into meat, leather and wool for the use of the unemployed was the objective of the FSRC. Millions of people were on a restricted diet, or in other words a diet capable of supporting life without any margin of safety. Meat prices rose, as they were bound to rise. Purchasing power lagged. Whatever food was to be had was that much food to the good. Of one grade or another, all of it inspected and passed as safe and edible, the Federal government had 657,396,312 pounds of dressed beef, all of which was to be given away.

During that period there were over 3,000,000 families on relief to whom was available, through their budgets, a maximum of twenty-five pounds a month. This compares with the fifty-eight pounds of meat a family eats when it has a diet of its choosing, in other words, a family at the top of the economic scale.

Eligible state institutions who received commodities had to make sworn affidavits that they were used in addition to their normal requirements. Our cotton, while we still had a mattress program, was made into mattresses for people who had not been able to replenish their household goods since perhaps long before 1929: Relief workers have seen them sleeping on coffinlike enclosures of sawdust, on springs covered with carpet, on the bare floor, on chairs put together. The women, sewing in workrooms, made sheets for people who had none, or who slept under flour sacks sewn together. They made clothes for families who had bought no clothes for years.

We received many representatives from interests who felt the FSRC was doing them out of legitimate business. On the contrary, the corporation resulted from an effort to save many agricultural producers from bankruptcy. It seems to me any scrutiny of the consuming power of the millions of potential purchasers who would enjoy a decent standard of living would convince any thoughtful man that here was no interference with the other end of the market.

CHAPTER IX

WORKS PROGRESS

Not only the farmer, but the city worker took on sharper characteristics as we looked at him more closely. We decided to learn as much as possible about these people on relief. How long had they been out of jobs? This would affect their re-employability, which, in turn, would not only determine the nature of a program designed to save or improve them as workers, but might indicate what likelihood there was of private industry absorbing these workers when the market opened up. We wanted to know which industries or occupations contributed most to the population on relief. We wanted to know what the respective places in the labor market of the colored and white races and their relative dependence on relief were. We wanted to know the comparative ages of employed and unemployed workers.

In the spring of 1934, we studied the workers on the relief rolls in seventy-nine cities. From that study emerged some facts which served to take the relief people out of the realm of unreality. We learned that the white collar class contributes a lower proportion of their workers to relief rolls than do the manual workers' classes in all kinds of industry.

We learned that one-fifth of all unemployed workers on relief were negroes—much more than their proportion in the privately employed population. In other words, negroes lost out faster than the white workers, a fact surprising to no one familiar with the chronic insecurity of negroes, or the small margin upon which they are forced to live, since they are customarily paid a lower wage than white workers for similar work similarly performed.

We learned that the typical unemployed city worker on relief was a white man, thirty-eight years of age and the head of a household, and that although his job history varied with his community, he had been more often than not an unskilled or semi-skilled worker in the manufacturing or mechanical industries. He had had some ten years' experience at what he considered to be his usual occupation. He had not finished elementary school. He had been out of any kind of job lasting one month or more for two years, and had not been working at his usual occupation for over two and a half years.

We learned that about three-fourths of these workers were men, and one-fourth women; that the men were, on the average, five years older than the women, and that both men and women were two years older than their fellow workers who still had jobs in private industry.

This matter of age is germane to the problem of dependence. We had decided arbitrarily not to consider as workers persons over sixty-four years and those under sixteen years of age. But within those years, when a man can be a legitimate competitor in the labor market, his age is a handicap more or less, according to whether he is skilled or unskilled. The unskilled man must be young, because the chief things he has to sell, besides his character, are his feet, back and arms. Therefore he gets an early start in the labor market where he displaces his elders before they are even middle-aged. This trend toward early displacement increases as industry relies more and more upon machines to do its skilled tasks and can turn to unskilled or semi-skilled human beings to do the rest. The impact of youth upon middle age is quickly felt on the relief rolls where the highest average age for men is found among the workers who used to be miners, or worked in factories or in mechanical industries.

If a man had part ownership in his job, this seemed to help him out. Draymen and teamsters, real estate agents, captains and mates, builders and contractors had been able to cling to independence until they were around forty-five. This age held also for such workers as marshals, sheriffs, railroad conductors and locomotive engineers in whom mature character is a saleable asset.

At the other end of the scale was the young man who couldn't get a job because he had never had a job, or at least not a job which would help him to a later career. He had delivered telegrams, blacked boots, sold newspapers. Almost an eighth of the total workers on relief in March, 1935, were without work experience of any kind and about two-thirds of these were between sixteen and twenty-five years of age.

Probably the average age of both the worker on relief as well as the worker in private industry has gone up since this study was made. Men cannot afford to retire, and have clung to their jobs, especially the skilled worker whose employers could not replace them easily. We know that the average relief worker has now been out of a job longer than he had been when this study was made. Even though a large turnover occurs on the relief rolls, and a given thousand on relief this month will not be the same thousand persons who were aided last month, it seems increasingly apparent that many of the working men and women who were mature when the depression began have, through hardship, discouragement and sickness as well as advancing years, gone into an occupational oblivion from which they will never be rescued by private industry.

This was the cloth to which we had to fit our pattern, or rather the pattern to which we had to fit our cloth. The working population, widely dismissed by the all-embracing term "people on relief," was broken up into much the same occupational groups as people off relief. Within these groups they were as used to individual ways of doing and thinking as was the world which was so willing to pass judgment on them. And I might add, they were just as honest, no less so; just as lazy, no lazier, than the rest of us.

To offer them a replica of the outside business world, if that had been desirable, was not in the cards. Policy from the first was not to compete with private business. Hence we could neither work on private property, set up a rival merchandising system, nor form a work outlet through manufacturing, even though manufacturing had contributed to relief rolls hundreds of thousands of workers accustomed to operating machines and to doing nothing else for a living.

Except for the National Youth Administration (and that, too, had a forerunner in our early student aid), the program which has been developed in the two and a half years since the close of CWA had its beginning in that fertile period when communities were figuring how to bring local benefits to pass with labor available through Federal funds. It has had no change of direction; it has been constantly diversified and enlarged.

Through our studies of the people on relief we were

able to get an idea of their special problems. One general program of direct relief was seen to be obviously inadequate in meeting the countless special groups on relief. We found that a large number of these people were employable—many of them skilled and many others with professional training. It seemed to us that the most intelligent way of providing relief to many of these people was through work relief. Many of the localities had initiated work relief projects during 1931, 1932 and 1933. FERA funds were used to support this work and we tried to improve the conditions of this work relief through the issuance of rules governing wages, hours, employment conditions and projects.

With the inauguration of the CWA the best of these local work relief projects were transferred to the CWA. Other projects, locally sponsored, initiated and supervised, were included under the CWA program. CWA projects were sponsored primarily by local governments and every attempt was made to fit the projects to the local people in need of work. The CWA was the first program to attempt diversification on a large scale and many skilled, professional and technical white collar workers in general obtained work at their usual occupation. Although most of the work performed under the CWA was of a construction type, we were able to provide special projects for clerical people, women, technicians, artists, doctors and nurses and other professional groups.

Although the CWA was of short duration, many of the projects were continued under the work relief program of the FERA. This program was inaugurated in March and April, 1934, after the CWA closed the major part of its work. The work relief program continued the general principle adopted during the CWA period, namely, to diversify work in order to provide the numerous occupational groups on relief with jobs in line with their training and experience. Localities were encouraged to initiate a variety of types of projects and we tried to pool the manifold experiences of the local units so as to stimulate local effort. This principle has been retained throughout our programs and under the WPA we have achieved greater diversification of work than on any of our earlier programs.

For fifteen months following CWA we returned to a work relief program whose scope and accomplishment is apt to be overlooked because it is overshadowed by WPA and because it was entered into at first by disappointed workers to whom CWA had been the brightest spot of the depression. During this period, a monthly average of nearly 2,000,000 persons were kept at work, and their physical accomplishments compared favorably with those of CWA, largely because CWA had turned up the ground. People everywhere were determined to keep up as much of the work as they could. Quality improved as citizens bettered the technique of locally instigated public work.

Partly because the limitations of work relief were reimposed, a unique record of Federal-state relationship was made in this year and a quarter. Federal funds allocated to the states were mingled with state funds and spent as such, both for direct and work relief. Each state government in turn dealt with county and local governments, with whose local funds it again mixed its own. The township control in New England, county control in some western states, and state departmental control in some southern states ultimately determined the pattern of work relief. Federal control, much looser than under CWA, was exercised by the giving or the withholding of grants. The actual operation of the program rested with the local governmental units.

The impossibility of conveying the full extent of accomplishments by enumerating them again makes me hesitate to give even a short summary of the work for which the American community is indebted to the unemployed people who were on relief in those months. They made or completely reconstructed 44,000 miles of roads, and repaired over 200,000 more. They built nearly 7,000 bridges; over 10,000 large culverts. They laid 2,700 miles of sanitary and storm sewers; dug more than 9,000 miles of drainage and irrigation ditches. They built 2,000 miles of levees, and laid over 1,000 miles of new water mains. They built 400 pumping stations. The country is 2,000 children's playgrounds, 800 parks, 350 swimming pools and 4,000 athletic fields to the good, because they were allowed to work rather than to receive straight relief.

During those months, however, pressure continued for a return to a work program that would take workers off relief. On April 8, 1935, the Emergency Relief Appropriation Act of 1935 was approved by the President, providing, among other things, for a Federal works program which included all emergency public works; the non-Federal projects of the PWA; the CCC; a Federal-state highway program under the Bureau of Public Roads and projects of regular Federal departments. Three new agencies (the Rural Electrification, the Resettlement, and the Works Progress Administrations) were set up in this enlarged plan of public works.

The WPA was to be the flexible unit acting to equalize employment on the larger projects. Its aim was to see that 3,500,000 persons were put to work at once on the entire works program. Because of this objective, WPA has favored those projects in which the proportion to be spent for labor is fairly high. Thus three factors govern the choice of projects. These are in order of their importance: First, the number of eligible relief workers in the locality; second, their skills; and third, the kind of project which will be of the greatest usefulness to the community. Thus, for instance, although a town may need a school badly, WPA will not build it unless the local labor reserve contains enough skilled construction workers. For these reasons WPA projects tend to be smaller than those of PWA which may have a larger materials ratio.

Under CWA only half the workers were taken from the relief rolls. Under WPA this proportion was raised to over 90 per cent. To insure proper supervisory ability and special skills, up to 10 per cent may be hired from persons not on relief. Prevailing wage rates are paid with a security monthly minimum which differs from region to region with living costs and habits. These prevailing rates are determined locally, and checked by the most reliable data on rates in private industry, construction and agriculture. Although we have by no means achieved it, there lies in our attempt the first approach to a security wage on an annual basis for any large group of workers.

The average Federal cost per man-year on WPA projects (inclusive of labor, materials and supplies) is approximately $780. The spread in actual man-year costs for labor alone is from around $350 in southeastern states to about $725 in high wage regions. About 80 per cent of Federal funds advanced goes for labor. The rest is added to those of the sponsor to buy materials and equipment. The ambitiousness of the job, therefore, is determined by the locality. One small city in Idaho which has a municipal power plant has matched funds out of its profits and has thus added to its public wealth. Administrative expense amounts to less than 4 per cent, although it is not static but varies with time and place, being necessarily higher at the outset.

As before, a construction program offered the best blanket answer to the abilities of the skilled and semi-skilled, especially since a large proportion of our skilled workers normally follows the building and construction trades. Therefore, the bulk of the WPA program has been a construction program. Farm-to-market roads have been our biggest job. Seventy per cent of American farmers take their produce to market, their children to school, get the doctor and the mail on dirt roads. To pull the farmer out of the mud, towns and villages and farmers' organizations sponsored projects valued at $168,000,000. Over 8,000 communities have built or repaired their water and sewer systems; some 6,000 have built and repaired their schools; 7,000 have erected or repaired other public buildings; nearly 170 installed or repaired electric utilities. Thousands of acres of malarial lands have been made habitable for people who have been long forced to live on or near them.

During this period we were to experience several natural disasters; floods in the East and West and two droughts, one of them the worst in recorded American history. At the moment of writing some 200,000 drought-stricken families are being taken care of in the drought area. On all work projects undertaken to give them wages emphasis is placed upon the conservation of water in a long-time land utilization program.

The collective effect of these and other physical

accomplishments upon American standards of living is hard to gauge. They can best be evaluated in the communities which wanted them enough to sponsor them, and whose local leadership determined the integrity of performance. There is a curious thing about these operations which have been dotting the landscape of the United States for the past three years. Although they are attacked constantly in newspapers, people who visit them report that workers, public officials and citizens alike exhibit strong pride in them. Derision is reserved for projects elsewhere that they have never seen.

A construction program, however, was no answer to the 400,000 unemployed women who were compelled to be the breadwinners of their families. It did not always prove true that these women knew much about domestic occupations. Many of them had been factory workers. Also their ignorance of home-making practice is a part of the level of education which accompanies their low living standards both as cause and effect. The bulk of the women's program, however, has been built around their traditional skills, and has taught thousands of women to make clothes, to can and to cook with knowledge of food values. The best of the thousands of sewing rooms are adapted to the varying stages of the skill of these 250,000 women who are sewing in them. Designed primarily to give them a wage, secondarily to make garments for people who would otherwise go without them, these women have made nearly 30,000,000 garments, individual and attractive enough so that they do not stigmatize the wearer as being on relief. The work is so geared that the least skilful, who are also apt to be timid, gain competence and self-confidence at the same time. Some of them are gaining professional skill at cutting and power machines, and will be able to take jobs in the garment industry.

The hot school lunch is another women's project. From one end of the country to the other, in crowded city schools and one-room school houses, women working for WPA have peeled the vegetables, cooked the hot dishes and poured the milk—the midday protective measure for children whose breakfasts and suppers are apt to be scant. Educators hope that the school lunch will remain as a device in social education. It should certainly never have to remain as a substitute for what parents should by right be able to give their children at home.

Some 9,000 women are engaged in bedside nursing and in public health. During the depression there was a breakdown of private health services all over the country. The percentage of patients cared for without charge rose from 15 to 60 per cent. As a consequence, Federal health projects had wide popularity. Over a thousand nurses and health workers were given Federal employment; clinics were opened; more than a million children were immunized against typhoid, diphtheria, smallpox and other infectious diseases, and tests to determine the presence of diphtheria, scarlet fever, tuberculosis and syphilis were made. As a result of this nation-wide campaign for health the professional people who carried it out have been re-employed either privately or as public servants in regions where the Federal work program demonstrated their value, and Federal health projects are now diminished in number. The consumer has learned of another way to purchase more life, and he is going to have it. This is but one indication of a point I should like to make in reference to all professional and service projects; that is, their tendency to create employment.

Among all these new service jobs, created to salvage workers rather than to create permanent work, the trend into permanent employment has been most pronounced among recreational workers. Within the next five years there should be many thousands of jobs opening up in the field of recreation. This is true, even with the current demand for recreation. Later, when there is more demand for his services, the recreation leader will become as necessary as the grade school teacher.

The American public in 1917 was shocked by the numbers of illiterate young men who turned out for the war. This was supposed to be the land of equal opportunity and the school house was the means of advancement. In a world conducted by the written sign, whether the sign is on a mile post, a bill of lading, or in a newspaper, it is hard to imagine the handicap under which a man must labor if he cannot read or write. He feels his exclusion even more if he has children in school, because his pride is involved. Over 250,000 grown men and women are taking this hurdle in literacy classes under teachers hired by WPA. In only one sense are literacy classes at the bottom of the educational program; they are the first means to an end. For a grown man to turn back to the beginning is an evidence of a thirst to read more than sign boards. His will to go to school in the first place must be pretty stubborn to keep him there. The volume and progress of the adult, parents' or workers' classes, are moving evidence of a collective determination to do something more about existence than submit to it. They want to master some of its problems and to enjoy being alive.

Most modern governments have conducted schools

for workers. Under the FERA and more fully developed under WPA they have been given government sponsorship for the first time in American history. Workers, many of them denied the privilege of
more than the most elementary schooling, are studying
their own problems, their place in history, and are dis-
cussing theories and practices of social, political and
economic organization.

The adult is not the only one who has lost out. The
children of the depression, many of them born into
homes already disorganized by want, have had their
childhood pressed and dented into a shape that resem-
bles childhood not at all. For the youngest ones nursery
schools were set up largely to acquaint them with
health routine.

What the depression has done to the youth of the nation we shall not know for many years. With not
enough food either to build healthy bodies, to stave off
sickness, to grow on, or even to stay the pangs of hunger; with not enough clothes to keep them warm or
clean, to say nothing of feeding their natural vanity;
living in homes of which they are ashamed and in
which they have neither privacy nor protection, they
have been ground between the millstones of want and
frustration. To the extent that the work program has
centered once more in the father the authority and
prestige which he had lost when out of work, and to
the extent that the family need has been diminished,
WPA has helped the young person. But not enough is
filtered down to help them in their individual per-
plexities. The National Youth Administration is only a
very partial answer to their problems. For one reason
there is insufficient money to touch more than a portion
of them, but it has enabled over 400,000 pupils to con-

tinue their schooling in high schools, colleges or graduate schools. It has given to others whose first necessity is a job third-time work and third-time wages on national projects in public service, research, recreation and community development. These useful fields offer to many of them their first experience with the discipline of work, since the labor market looks indifferently upon their eagerness to get a job.

The largest part of our white collar workers come from the business and not from the professional world. They form a flexible labor supply to undertake on an important scale research basic to future governmental policies. Under the supervision of specialists in Federal departments they are gathering information to fill gaps in our social knowledge, which previously had to be supplied by small regular staffs, or by a few brave scholars and a handful of student investigators. We have only begun as a nation to be self-critical; to learn how we live, what we live by, and how we can improve our lot. Research is popular in the United States. Business pays highly for it, and frequently endows research with or without hope of profit. Yet for lack of analysis as to the social significance of his occupation, people are using the WPA investigator as the ultimate boondoggler, his foot in the door, his pencil on his pad. We are examining our social system with the very workers which the system threw out. They are studying, among other things, chronic diseases, facts about housing, occupational characteristics, and unemployment. The return on this investment is such that much of the work is apt to be taken on as a regular function. We can afford to pay to know something about ourselves.

Notwithstanding the almost immeasurable benefits

that will accrue to the public from the physical labors of the unemployed, I have come to the belief that the greatest contributions, not only to American life and culture, but to employment, are these less tangible ones made by our professional and service workers. If it is more ironical for one person to be on relief than another it is seen in the fact that scientists, nurses, artists, architects, painters, economists, writers, musicians and all the rest of those persons, who by virtue of gifts and discipline have arrived in that upper fraction of the people who lead the way of history, should find themselves without recognition, livelihood, or any means to continue the benefits which only they can bestow. It is said that the profit of business lies in the last 8 per cent of its volume. The profit of our social experience certainly lies in the hands of a very small minority. That WPA has been the vehicle for this group to pursue their work, not for the privileged few alone, as they have been able to do in the past, but for public benefit, establishing in some ways a new base for American life, is a fact of which we can be very proud. Throughout history, nations have set their approval upon the practices of the arts and sciences by making them the reward of the few. Government is now taking a hand on behalf of the many. Still predicating its program only on the right of the worker to his living, the Federal government, through the agency of WPA, has extended its encouragement of the arts. Writers, architects, painters, workers in the graphic arts, sculptors, musicians, actors, dramatists, composers and producers, encouraged and trained by the leading men in their fields, have participated in a program that has used every relationship of the artist to his material, and of teacher to pupil, except where it would trespass on the normal private transactions of professionally paid workers.

In its entire range, from alphabet to gym work, to chamber music, art exhibits, and murals on hospital walls, this program is the advance agent of a potential industry; one which will be a large-scale employer and will cater to the demands of workers to service the needs of literally millions of new consumers. Few things could add such a permanent volume of employment as would a program of educating the public to use the services and participate in the pleasures of the culture we possess. I use the word culture here as including everything from basketball to a violin performance. Its practicability as a potential employing device makes more amazing the ridicule that was at first heaped upon it. This ridicule is fast abating and one now finds the metropolitan élite at WPA "first nights" because they expect to find there both fine performance and new subject matter. The volume of public response to painting has astonished practically everyone connected with the Federal Art Project. Painters cannot keep up with the demand for pictures. Therapeutists in hospitals call for murals. Painting classes are demanded widely. As for the living theatre, it is doubtful if even its enthusiasts expected such response. So great is the audiences' longing to see real people on the stage that the quality of the performance does not affect their enjoyment. People in the country will travel miles to see a rather badly done play or vaudeville entertainment, and go home pleased. The stimulus of such responsive audiences is strongly felt by actors whose performance greatly improves when talented supervisors can be found.

Of course, other factors than depression and the Federal Music Project enter into the current musical revival. When mechanical music first made its appearance, boys and girls abandoned the piano. Musical movies and the radio displaced many orchestras. The result of widespread exposure of the public to ready-made music has been quite the reverse of popular expectation. Radio has fostered both musical appreciation and ambition to make music. Manufacturers of phonograph records report an unprecedented volume of demand for classical music. Music publishers also announce the same increased interest in orchestral scores. The Federal Music Project thus had much to contribute and nothing to resist in the current trend except the inherent difficulties of producing good music. With the aid of the best conductors and teachers taken from non-relief sources to enhance the musical quality of the organizations, there have been many performances of first rank, approved by critics and audiences alike. Not alone in symphony halls, parks and schools but even in railway stations, people have listened to music at first-hand who have before been kept away by price. During seven months of last year over a million and a half persons in New York alone heard Federal programs and concerts. In Mississippi 69,000 people attended music classes taught by over 100 Federal music teachers. Much of this work will be taken over by the states or the community; already this trend is emerging.

The position of writers in the democratization of culture is harder to gauge. Under WPA they have been used to prepare *The American Guide*, a labor of such monumental proportion that no publisher could undertake it, though its compilation was widely desired. The historical significance of this publication is already ap-

parent, and there is always the possibility, of course, that due to history's bondage to the written word it will be one of our boasted accomplishments to survive us. The future of the writer not as artist, but as employee, perhaps will be determined by our attitude toward literacy. With thousands of new literates, one would expect that in addition to the paper manufacturers, the publishers, the editors, the newsboys and the printer's devil, the authors, too, should rejoice.

This renascence of the arts, if we can call it a rebirth when it has no precedent in our history, was perhaps due to arrive through the suffering and discipline of these recent years. It certainly betokens a deep spiritual change and re-estimate of what is valuable in American life. WPA has done no more than to assist it. But the volume of the production which WPA has made possible, springing up as it has spontaneously in all parts of the country, has more than an accidental relationship to its quality, just as major literature, painting, sculpture, music and drama is work of scope and magnificence. The quickening of the audience, the new desire to fill life with something more than the competitive struggle for existence, undoubtedly accelerates the process. And this demand itself, both on the part of the performer and the one who enjoys the performance, points to a new upward movement of labor.

If leisure, once the privilege only of the rich, is now to belong to everybody, one objective of any move to share the world's wealth has already been accomplished. It would be curious if we found that the mastering and enjoyment of this leisure, which was forced upon us under such economic stress, would be one of the means of easing that same stress. Often in the past we have turned to blood-letting for unemploy-

ment. Besides famine and disease war has been our handiest depopulator. We have thought of less rather than more life as a way out of the conundrums which mechanical progress keeps always on the desk of government. We have tried colonial expansion in every direction but upward; sideward for new land, downward by decimation. A mass impetus upward may prove to be more than an equivalent for war.

This is the work. What is left to be done I have indicated by showing only its beginning. We have turned over the American board and seen how many people live like slugs beneath its plenty. We have seen also what hundreds of thousands of people are stretching toward the life of the spirit, from the middle-aged man who is learning to spell his name to the WPA sculptor who went without bread and spent his security wage on a piece of stone. The regeneration of the individual worker no longer needs to be the only concern of a national work program for the unemployed. We have come to a second concept which is that his work is necessary to enrich the national life. In adopting this second principle we have not, however, abandoned our first. Our work must be work for the worker by the worker. He is the first figure. He must be the first and last digit in all government accounting.

CHAPTER X

THE OUTLOOK

AMERICA has spent the last few years in the counting house. Only a few will say we have been counting out our money only. We have counted our national wealth and our national income. We have counted our poverty, and I have tried here to give a part of the new audit. We have measured our will and our intelligence. From our inventory we have emerged, as a nation, with the conviction that there is no need for any American to be destitute, to be illiterate, to be reduced by the bondage of these things into either political or economic impotence.

We are sometimes accused of stirring up class hatreds when we say such things. On the contrary, I believe that under national scrutiny all Americans are revealed as Americans, with rights as well as obligations; that there is coming out of our new knowledge of who Americans are and how they live a reunion of forces which had flown so far apart that they no longer knew each other.

The ways by which more and more people can have their rightful share of the national income I shall leave to the experts, the legislators, and to forces of labor who are intent on bringing this about. If we had no other reason for it than to keep the system going, ways would have to be figured out by which the worker could buy back his full share of the goods he helped to put through the mill of national business.

There is, however, another way of looking at it. One may believe that the human being should come first, and the serviceability of the economic system in which he functions should be estimated by the number of persons who share in its rewards. There is reason to think that the present system is capable of giving to all its workers those things which are now the expectations of a comparative few: a warm, decent place to live in; a liberal diet; suitable clothes; travel, vacations, automobiles, radios, and college educations for those who want them. Even one who does not pretend to be an expert on the subject can see a few fairly obvious means by which we can approach the problem of redistribution. Wages must be raised and hours lowered. Unfair profits will have to be translated into lower unit price. Some three million persons over sixty years of age should be taken out of the labor market. Most of them are there not because they want to be, but from dire necessity. Compulsory school age, with some exceptions, probably should be raised, and young boys removed from competition with their fathers.

Until the time comes, if it ever does, when industry and business can absorb all able-bodied workers—and that time seems to grow more distant with improvements in management and technology—we shall have with us large numbers of unemployed. Intelligent people have long since left behind them the notion that under fullest recovery, and even with improved purchasing power, the unemployed will disappear as dramatically as they made their appearance after 1929.

Even if they did so disappear, there would still remain with us the people who cannot work, or should not, and who have no one to support them; the too old, the too young, mothers with small children, the sick and crippled. These people cannot be left to fumble their way along alone; to be sent from one vacillating agency to another, given something one month and not the next, with almost nothing in the present and, so far as they know, nothing at all in the future. For them a security program is the only answer. In the past three and a half years more progress has been made in providing security for them than during the whole history of the nation. The Social Security Board has been set up; appropriations have been made, public education has begun, but most important, over one million unemployable persons are already receiving its benefits. We need only to refine, extend and consolidate gains that have been made in order to provide minimum security for all of them.

Many who wanted the continuance of Federal relief by grants in aid to states, contended that if you gave unemployable people back to the care of the states, they would be neglected. In some places, even widely, this has proved to be true. States should never pass them on to the niggardly and degrading practices of county and township poor relief. Federal aid, I believe, should be given through the Social Security Board which, with similar state and local boards, should pass this benefit as a pension without stigma to those who need it. If this is to be done, it is equally clear that the Social Security Board must be given power to regulate standards of administration in states and cities. Too small a benefit will not serve the purpose of a pension. Political control of the manner in which it is administered would destroy it. An adequate civil service made up of permanent employees is absolutely essential to the success of any pension system.

Assurance as to the source of such large sums is of paramount importance. At the present time, because it makes initial expenditures, the local community determines the amount of pensions. As I have said before, local funds in the main come from a tax on real estate. For an enlarging program of inevitably increasing outgo, the real estate tax is too thin a reed to lean upon. We should at once consider coordination of tax methods to assure a fair and equitable distribution of the tax base.

There will remain, however, as the responsibility of government, a standing army of able-bodied workers who have no jobs. Probably for years to come it will be an army of substantial size. It will be flexible, increasing and decreasing with seasons, with changes in production habits and industrial geography, but chiefly, until we have vanquished it, changing with cyclical unemployment. If we keep it in training so that only by sickness or old age will its members lapse into unemployability, it can be a reserve drawn upon by private undertakings at any time they need new labor and are willing to pay the going wage for it. Private businesses or industries, however, cannot be asked to keep upon their payrolls large numbers of workers whom they cannot use.

What is the outlook for these unemployed? First, workers must have unemployment insurance. This is part of any social security program. An insurance benefit, however, will not tide a man through an indefinite period of unemployment. Nor will it take care of the annual net increase of over 400,000 workers who come of age each year, and the other young who have never had jobs. It will not take care of the casual laborer, the agricultural or the household worker. The Social Security Act potentially covers only about half the workers in the nation. One of the first necessities is to see if it cannot be given greater coverage.

To me, the only possible solution for those who cannot be absorbed by long-time or large-scale public works is a work program. I believe we must continue such a program until other forces produce a very substantial increase in the volume of employment. Some people would like to turn the unemployed back to the communities. Others advocate restoration of Federal relief. They would permit local governments to share the cost, but they would give local governments complete discretion as to the size and the character of the benefit. What we might expect of such a benefit, how large it would be and in what manner administered has already been indicated to us by the fate of many unemployables who have already suffered from it.

Behind their arguments is a natural desire to make unemployment relief cheaper. There is widespread feeling that by some mysterious means an unemployed person will not eat so much or require such warm clothes if his relief is given by the local community as if it were given through a Federal plan in cooperation with states or municipalities. Granted that direct relief is cheaper, the nation will get no return on its money if it goes back to direct relief. We shall go through the gesture of keeping people alive. For all its tremendous natural wealth, the American people are the greatest resource of the country. So far men and women, with few exceptions, have found no substitute for useful work to keep themselves sound of body and mind. In other words, work conserves them as a national asset, and lack of work lets them sink into a national liability.

Once again, however, there are two sides to the story. The unemployed need work, the public needs construction done and services rendered which neither private business nor regular departments of government are in a position to undertake. What the public thinks of their accomplishment is revealed in the character of groups who instigate or sponsor projects to the extent of putting up the money for their material costs and of assuring responsibility for their execution. When CWA was started, doubt was expressed in many quarters as to whether the tasks would hold out, yet new ones were brought forward with increasing speed and urgency. As corroboration of public demand, the National Conference of Mayors has asked for a continuance of a program which has already added millions of dollars of wealth to their cities. In many small towns and rural areas it is claimed that WPA projects have advanced the standards of living by fifty years. Communities now find themselves in possession of improvements which even in 1929 they would have thought themselves presumptuous to dream of.

In fact, everywhere there has been an overhauling of the word presumptuous. We are beginning to wonder if it is not presumptuous to take for granted that some people should have much, and some should have nothing; that some people are less important than others and should die earlier; that the children of the comfortable should be taller and fatter, as a matter of right, than the children of the poor.

It finally whittles itself down, I suppose, to a matter of the children, since we ourselves are not likely to see all those ends accomplished toward which we strive. Suppose we place two grown men beside each other. One has been given all the privileges of his time, and has made good use of them; the other has never had a glimpse of privilege. The first is healthy; the second sick from neglect. If we were told that one was going to be abandoned, and the other encouraged to carry on, which one should we choose to keep? In a democracy, no matter how conspicuously we fail to operate upon the principle, we don't admit that one man has more right to live than another. Yet realistically, it would be easy to say which is the more useful member of society.

Put two children in their place. Upon one child privilege has only started to take effect. Neglect of the other has scarcely begun. How shall the choice be made between them, and who will dare to be the chooser?

INDEX

187

AMERICANA LIBRARY

The City: The Hope of Democracy
By Frederic C. Howe
With a new introduction by Otis A. Pease

Bourbon Democracy of the Middle West, 1865–1896
By Horace Samuel Merrill
With a new introduction by the author

*The Deflation of American Ideals: An Ethical Guide
for New Dealers*
By Edgar Kemler
With a new introduction by Otis L. Graham, Jr.

Borah of Idaho
By Claudius O. Johnson
With a new introduction by the author

The Fight for Conservation
By Gifford Pinchot
With a new introduction by Gerald D. Nash

Upbuilders
By Lincoln Steffens
With a new introduction by Earl Pomeroy

The Progressive Movement
By Benjamin Parke De Witt
With a new introduction by Arthur Mann

*Coxey's Army: A Study of the
Industrial Army Movement of 1894*
By Donald L. McMurry
With a new introduction by John D. Hicks

*Jack London and His Times: An Unconventional
Biography*
By Joan London
With a new introduction by the author

San Francisco's Literary Frontier
By Franklin Walker
With a new introduction by the author

The Liberal Republican Movement
By Earle D. Ross
With a new introduction by John G. Sproat

Growth and Decadence of Constitutional Government
By J. Allen Smith
With a new introduction by Dennis L Thompson

Breaking New Ground
By Gifford Pinchot
With a new introduction by James Penick, Jr.

Spending to Save: The Complete Story of Relief
By Harry L. Hopkins
With a new introduction by Roger Daniels

A Victorian in the Modern World
By Hutchins Hapgood
With a new introduction by Robert Allen Skotheim

The Casual Laborer and Other Essays
By Carleton H. Parker
With a new introduction by Harold M. Hyman